THE STORIED SEA

SUSAN E. WALLACE

CRAWFORDSVILLE
GENERAL LEW WALLACE
STUDY & MUSEUM
2015

Commemorative edition © 2015 Lew Wallace Study
Preservation Society

Direct inquiries to:
    General Lew Wallace Study & Museum
    P.O. Box 662
    Crawfordsville, IN 47933
    study@ben-hur.com
    www.ben-hur.com

Wallace, Susan E. (Susan Elston), 1830-1907
    The Storied Sea / Susan E. Wallace.
    ISBN: 978-0-9863774-0-2

First edition--1883, Boston: James R. Osgood and
Company

NOTE FROM THE DIRECTOR

At the General Lew Wallace Study & Museum we are committed to the protection and preservation of Lew Wallace's legacy. As part of our mandate we also seek to celebrate a belief in the power of the individual spirit to affect American history and culture. It would be impossible for us to preserve the legacy of Lew Wallace and share our mandate without recognizing the incredible impact that Susan Wallace had on Lew's life and achievements.

Lew and Susan were devoted to each other throughout their 53 years of marriage. While Susan often deferred to her husband, she was truly a partner in all aspects of their relationship. It was Susan who brought Lew to Crawfordsville in 1853, a place he would call home for over 50 years. She followed him on assignments and postings during his military, political, and diplomatic careers. She also served as a sounding board for his writings and speeches. While she exercised some influence over Lew, she clearly encouraged Lew to embrace his creativity and individuality—which must have been difficult for her at times.

Beyond her devotion to Lew, Susan had a writing career of her own, was active in the temperance movement, and was instrumental in the preservation of the New Mexican archives. Prior to the release of *Ben-Hur* in 1880, Susan was arguably as well known for her writing as Lew. She was a witty, insightful and thoughtful writer who was featured in some of the most important periodicals of the 19th century in addition to the publication of her individual works.

When looking at the sum total of his life, it is clear that Susan Elston Wallace was the person who most influenced her husband, Lew. It would be impossible to consider the life and impact he had without celebrating her life and accomplishments as well. It is a great honor and obligation to keep the legacy of Susan Wallace alive, even as we remember Lew.

Larry Paarlberg
Executive Director
General Lew Wallace Study & Museum

EDITORIAL NOTE

The staff of the General Lew Wallace Study & Museum have reproduced Susan Wallace's words in this volume as faithfully as possible. All spellings, grammatical errors, and word usage are hers. We chose not to mark these with a [sic] to avoid interrupting the flow of the narrative. As a result, the reader will notice words such as Niarara instead of Niagara, cimeter, which is today spelled scimitar, and pedler--today spelled peddler. Susan also refers to Istanbul as Istamboul or Stamboul. The first edition of *The Storied Sea* was published in 1883 by James R. Osgood and Company of Boston. This Lew Wallace Study Preservation Society commemorative edition is being published as part of our Hoosier Bicentennial project, culminating with our 2016 exhibit on Hoosier authors.

"There it is, at last, -- the long line of heavenly blue, and over it, far away, the white-peaked lateen sails; and there, close to the rail, beyond the sand-hills, delicate wavelets are breaking forever on a yellow beach, each in exactly the same place as the one which fell before. One glance shows us children of the Atlantic that we are on a tideless sea.

"There it is, -- the sacred sea. The sea of all civilization, and almost all history, girdled by the fairest countries in the world; set there that human beings from all its shores might mingle with each other, and become humane, -- the sea of Egypt, of Palestine, of Greece, of Italy, of Byzant, of Marseilles, and this Narbonnaise, 'more Roman than Rome herself,' to which we owe the greater part of our own progress; the sea too of Algeria, and Carthage, and Cyrene, and fair lands now desolate, surely not to be desolate forever, -- the sea of civilization. Not only to the Christian, nor to the classic scholar, but to every man to whom the progress of his race from barbarism to humanity is dear, should the Mediterranean Sea be one of the most august and precious objects on this globe; and the first sight of it should inspire reverence and delight, as of coming home, -- home to a rich inheritance, in which he has long believed by hearsay, but which he sees at last with his own mortal corporal eyes."

-- Prose Idylls, Charles Kingsley.

PREFACE.

ADDRESSED by the author to the beloved unseen reader who wrote asking that these newspaper letters might be collected into a book.

Through the courtesy of the editor of the "New York Independent," I now have the opportunity; and it is a deep pleasure to think that in this new dress I shall be recognized and welcomed as an old acquaintance. As indicated in my initial chapter, I have not tried to entertain the privileged few "who have everything," but have sought to amuse those whose recreations are not many, -- the poor and the sick, the sorry and the dissatisfied. This last is a pale procession, like the innumerable company John saw, which no man could number for multitude. In the summer voyage, very precious to me, among my unseen friends have been the bride in Nebraska who denied herself butter for a season that she might subscribe to the "Independent," and the young girl in Vermont who wants to know why she, who loves poetry so well, cannot write it. Nor have I strained to be instructive. Schools and libraries are crammed with useful knowledge, and the hackneyed sights of the Elder World may be paved with ponderous volumes of accurate description of the "shining Orient." I have aimed only at an easy familiarity of talk, such as we would have together should we meet, as I hope we may, some happy morning. The guide-book is for the student of facts, -- let me refer you to Baedeker and Murray, -- but these transient pictures in water are for the gentle, patient soul wanting rest from that weariness known in our dear native land as mental culture.

Parting is sweet sorrow to lovers whispering in the starlit stillness of Italian nights, but not to us no longer young. In the shadows of mature years wistfully we ask, When, where, how, shall we meet again? So it is with feeling akin to pain I say good-by. The reader, so often addressed as "dear," is not a phantom or a shade, but a constant companion grown into an abiding presence. It is not possible to dismiss such comradeship without regret. To all who have sent pleasant messages across the seas, peace and health!

SUSAN E. WALLACE.

Constantinople, May 1, 1883.

CONTENTS

I. ON THE SEA

AT first I was wofully seasick. A violent wind-storm came on, as we left Genoa, and, after the rack of twenty hours of misery, I gathered together the wretched remains of a body once fondly called my own and dragged it up on deck, in the hope that favoring winds might smooth the worn face to something less like the tangled lines of a map of a railroad centre. The "Fleur de Luce" is the flower of French steamers, new and clean, tidy and bright; the staterooms full of snug little contrivances, pockets and shelves, for the comfort of passengers. The captain, in fresh uniform, was an ancient mariner, with frosty whiskers and a fruit-like bloom in his cheeks; the very ideal of a commandant, and wearing the sweet courtesy which makes his nation the most attractive to the stranger of any people in the world. He came, without introduction, to say he was charmed, "and every one on board is, also, to see Madame on deck." Madame strove to frame a gracious answer, from detached and faded recollections of Oilendorf, rounding it with a ghastly but appreciative smile. "As there are but two ladies in the 'Fleur de Luce,' it would be a shame to have them *ennuye* one moment."

He glanced admiringly at the fair, sweet face beside me, and was repaid with a smile that was better than others' speech, and a few timid words, gently spoken, in Indiana French. The captain of an American vessel would have smiled at English so imperfectly worded; but the Frenchman never wounds one's *amour proper*.

"There!" exclaimed the dapper little man, with a quick, energetic movement, which displaced the Provence rose in his button-hole. "Do you see that pale blue line?"

I looked down the gold-laced sleeve and sunburnt finger, in the direction pointed, and saw nothing but a sky that would be dazzling were it not so soft, and the sea, showing yet the dread swell of the storm in its flecks of foam.

"If Madame will have the goodness to look through the glass, she will sight the Island of Corsica."

I adjusted the lens to my failing vision, and lo! in faintest, dying hues the hills which the man who shook the world with his armies must have trodden when a boy. It was what the genial captain had intended, -- a diversion, or, as the French put it, a "distraction." My ills were forgotten. I saw the birthplace of Napoleon. Restoring the glass to its owner, who bowed briskly and as briskly walked away, my next thought was to take from my capacious ulster pocket a tiny scratch-book, free of any memorandum, and a new pencil, attached to it by a string of red tape. Resting the book on my knee, I proceeded to make an entry on what an old-time poet might call its virgin page.

"Surely," said Thalia, looking up from crochet, "you are not going to attempt anything about the Mediterranean. Why, it has been written over for four thousand years."

"Dear Thalia," I replied mildly, but with the firmness becoming the advocate of universal suffrage, "there was once an artist whom the sons of men named The Divine. He had painted a hundred Madonnas, and one day he spread a canvas and poured magic colors on his palette for the one hundred and first Holy Mary. Just then the judicious friend, who is never far off, entered the famous studio. 'What!' he exclaimed, astonished. 'Another Madonna!' Said Raphael, with the rapt gaze which makes his face like the face of the archangel whose name he bears, 'if all the artists of all the world should spend their lives in painting the Blessed Virgin, they could never exhaust her beauty.' So of this fairest of seas."

"I understand," said Thalia, pettishly. "You would add a story to the Tower of Babel."

It must be admitted travel is a hard strain on the temper. Many a match has been broken off and many a warm friend cooled in the ups and downs of the most comfortable journeyings. We two, usually in absolute harmony, were out of tune. I, worn and haggard with seasickness; she gay and charming, insisting it was all nonsense, in her pride of stomach looking with deep contempt on the ignoble mind which basely yielded to the spirits of the vasty deep.

"Thalia," I replied, in bitterness of soul, "wisdom will die with you. Suppose I should indulge that lofty ambition you hint of, there are those who might watch my struggles heavenward and read the report with interest, -- young people, to whom this world is not worn out, in fact, is something new, and life sweet and unspoiled."

Thalia is not so young as she once was, and I touched her there, not intending it.

"You know," I said, taking courage while I cut the fresh lead-pencil with an equally fresh pocket-knife, "in our own dear native land there are eighty thousand school-teachers."

"I know. Once I was in that noble army of martyrs myself."

"I remember. They are between the upper and nether millstone; underpaid and overworked; slaves of a system, part of a boasted machine which stops not day nor night. They are mainly women, young girls, with hungry minds and weary bodies, and their best recreation is reading. On chintz lounges, cheap and hard, they lay their aching and breaking backs, and in short hours of rest snatch up something to read which tells of scenes unlike as possible to the dull grind of their daily duty. The Mediterranean is not stale and hackneyed to them. For them I sing" (loftily); "not for women with health, wealth, ease, who in evenings have only to sit in a too easy chair and watch the firelight play on diamonds." And I glanced at a superb solitaire following the crochet-needle.

Thalia shook a cinder from her knitting and was silent. I pursued my subject. "There are young mothers rocking the cradle -- of future senators, let us hope -- who may like to hear the old tales of the storied sea; and farmers' boys, possible Presidents, ploughing in work so uncongenial that the Mississippi Valley is a valley of dry bones to them, instead of a land flowing with milk and honey, the glory of all lands. Why is it that the humdrum clerk, chained to the counter of a country 'store,' and the telegraph boy, in the railroad station of the out townships, revel in tales of Buffalo Bill, the Scalp-Hunters of Bloody Gulch, and the Sleuth-Hound of the Sierras?"

"I suppose," said Thalia, thoughtfully, "they want a contrast."

"Precisely." I waved my scratch-book triumphantly, and began quoting my paper before the Indianapolis Culture Club. "There are thousands of women who are living, and will die before long, in narrow ruts, who long to see the world, but cannot

4

look beyond the limits of their own State, except with others' eyes. Sunburnt, flat-chested, high-shouldered farmers' wives, who, from rosy youth to wrinkled age, vibrate between nursery and kitchen; patient women, with hard hands and soft hearts, whose unwritten lives bear a pathos unspeakable, -- they have buried the early wishes, hopelessly cherished, now ineffably dear, like the memory of dead children. The passionate longing has faded into a tender, lingering regret. It has no sting, because women learn readily to accept the inevitable; but the trace of that feeling will never be quite effaced. In their half-hours of leisure they sit in the summer twilight, not lighting the lamps for fear of drawing mosquitoes, and dream of a lost time in dim Arcadian days, when they believed it possible they too might hear the 'Miserere,' the music which makes men tremble and women faint, and listen to the curlew's cry above the blue Symplegades. They have 'given up,' and know that the hour will never come which brings them even so far as the shades of Mammoth Cave or within the thrill of the mighty voice of Niarara. Their biographies are forever unwritten; only the seer, looking below the surface, can guess what still, deep currents ebb and flow beneath the moveless calm. No wonder the insane asylums are recruited from the farm-houses."

"No wonder," echoed Thalia, softly, laying down her work and absently looking at the shore of Ajaccio. "My mother was such a woman. She brought up six riotous children in a daily struggle to make both ends meet. That she did not go crazy was because her strong will and love of books carried her over the bridge from which so many in those straits fall. She used to read the foreign letters of the 'Post' and the New York 'Tribune,' sitting by the oven door, as she browned the coffee and baked bread, and never tired of Irving and the old travellers and of hearing the missionaries talk.

When we children used to sing 'Jerusalem the Golden,' how many times I have heard her say, 'Oh, if I could only see the City of David!' But she died without the sight."

Tears started to the blue eyes, at which I shook my head. "No tears for her, my dear. The New Jerusalem is better than the Old. Perhaps, if she were here, she might read what I have to say about Olivet and Calvary." Thalia nodded. "And then," to resume, "there are pale sempstresses, like Maud Muller by the spring, longing for something better than she had known (another sentence from the aforenamed essay); for her I sing, and, besides, -- and this is the strongest plea for new letters on stale subjects, -- no two persons see eye to eye, and there is freshness in every first view. You have seen the 'Lady of Lyons'?"

"I have," said Thalia, brightening at the recollection, -- "in bridal beauty listening to the voice of the charmer charming never so wisely, -- and I cried my handkerchief full when she said, 'Tell him for years I never nursed a thought that was not his.'" And Thalia rose to her feet and repeated in a little sing-song that lovely passage.

"I saw her, too, in her own Lyons." She fell into a listening, pensive attitude. "It was at the close of a long, hot dusty day, and down by the river which rushes past the silk-weaver's chimneys. She wore an absurd cap, made like a boy's flutter-mill, which flapped in the wind over her freckled forehead. My Pauline was tall and broad, fat and busy, her cheeks tanned to a dead-leaf brown. Her black stuff dress was tucked up to the waist, showing legs shaped like milestones and as sturdy."

"How you do love to spoil things!" said Thalia, indignantly. "I did not see her."

"No; you were in a warm nap, maybe, dreaming of Pauline at McVicar's, where she appears

"I tell you of the Lady of Lyons as I saw her, -- the daughter of the dirty city, her foot, a number six, on her native heath, and her hand in the dye-tub."

"Horrid woman! Not in the dye?"

"That is where the genuine Pauline appears in the true picture; all the rest are counterfeits. Her elbows were streaked with various colors, and she washed a skein of yarn in the stream which colored her hands red as Lady Macbeth's. They will never whiten."

"How different truth is from poetry," said Thalia, regretfully, "and how unlike the sympathetic see!"

"You illustrate my text perfectly. Then I have your consent to attempt a fleeting picture in these water-colors, have I?"

"Well"(reluctantly), "you may, under promise that you keep clear of that old hack." And she gave the red-backed Baedeker a sharp hit with the ivory needle.

"I promise, and you and the rest of my friends remember you hold the reserved right of not reading what the latest pilgrim has to tell."

We lay back in our comfortable ship-chairs, and the steamer held on toward the shining shore.

"One thing more," said Thalia, lifting her voice. "For pity's sake, don't copy the accurate-figures traveller, who saw the Sphinx at eleven o'clock. August 21, 1875, and climbed up a ladder with 10,000 rounds and measured its nose, and it was exactly five feet and six inches long."

"I shall avoid all accurate figures with the utmost ease and pleasure, and also the style of the deeper borer, who makes a journal in this wise: --

"After a restless night, rose and looked out. Weather rainy and cold.

"'*October 9.* Bad weather still continues.

"*October 10.* Signs of clearing, but misty and dull.

"*October 11.* Bright but chilly. Will visit the Hebrides to-morrow.

"*October 12.* Fog came up and ruined the day's excursion,' etc."

We laughed together, for the first time in two days. "To thine own self be true, my Thalia, and I will be to mine, and will submit every line to your criticism."

"No, no. Take any shape but that," she cried, with tragic gesture, "and my firm nerves shall never tremble. But here we are at Ajaccio."

Dear reader, you do not know, you never can know, till we change places, how glad I am to catch your friendly eyes again. The sights are but half seen, the sounds but half heard, without you. Your grace and favor have warmed my heart, and your sympathy and kind words have been to me golden harvests of garnered sheaves. Let me hold your hand while we stumble along the rugged mountain-side, and in the warm valleys, strewn with sculptured stones, each one a history. Not on the sea alone, but in many a narrow crossing, shall I sing, --

"TAKE, O BOATMAN, THRICE THY FEE, --
TAKE, I GIVE IT WILLINGLY;
FOR, INVISIBLE TO THEE,
SPIRITS TWAIN HAVE CROSSED WITH ME."

II. THE MAN OF DESTINY

I HAVE seen the chapels, mosques, and temples of the farthest East, the red minarets of Cairo, and the vari-colored shades of the Alhambra; but nothing has ever touched me like the tomb of Napoleon, in Paris. It is a perfect harmony, charming the eye as exquisite music holds the ear. "The place of his rest is glorious," I said, as I entered the marble church of the Hôtel des Invalides, shaped like the dome of our own Capitol. The stillness and coolness of the great chamber after the glare of the white, hot streets was solemn and soothing to the tired sense. The tombs of the faithful Duroc and Bertrand passed, then we bent over the marble balustrade and looked down in the spacious circular crypt, with its awful sarcophagus of black marble, which contains the lead and cedar coffins of St. Helena. It holds all that is left of the Man of Destiny. A rush of feeling came over me, as a strong wave bears you off your feet, and tears started to my eyes with the mere sense of the beautiful. The twelve lamps, of Pompeiian bronze, lighted the space and gilded chapel above. The tessellated pavement was a crown of laurel, set with stripes; rays, forming a star, breaking from the wreath which surrounds the monument. In that costly pavement read the enchanted names: Kivoli, the Pyramids, Marengo, Austerlitz, Jena, Friedland, Wagram, Moscowa. They stir the blood, like notes of the bugle calling to battle. The flags from those fields are there, drooping shreds and tatters of the splendid banners that flew but to victory; a pathetic history. Descend the steps and mark a slab of black marble above the stately brass gate which closes the dark peristyle. On it are engraved these words, from the Emperor's will: --

"I DESIRE THAT MY ASHES MAY REST
ON THE BANKS OF THE SEINE,
AMONG THAT FRENCH NATION I LOVED SO WELL."

On each side the gate is a colossal brass statue. One holds the globe, the other the imperial sceptre. They seem to guard the sleep of the greatest modern captain and hold his fame in silent and eternal keeping. In the sword-room, reached by a gate of gilt bronze, are sixty standards, the records of triumphant fields, the golden crown given by the town of Cherbourg, the badges and sword of Austerlitz. They appeal to Frenchmen yet with undiminished force, and even to the stranger.

What a strange doom that of all that fighting family only one, a remote descendant, should die in battle! Poor little Louis! Unhappy Eugenie! It was hardly a battle, either; a skirmish with savages in a barbarian province, where the gentle boy thought to win his spurs, and with them, perhaps, the hand of an English princess. What a tender souvenir was his will, and, oh! what towering hopes were laid away in his untimely grave!

The harbor of Ajaccio is a curve, graceful as a bent bow. First it was but mist, vapor; then the quay; then blue hills back of the town, which lies close to the water's edge. Built of white stone and glistening like snow in the noonday sun, it had the air of neatness and thrift characteristic of nearly all French towns, refreshing the mind and imagination of the housekeeper. One reason is, stone houses do not show age like the pine boxes we live in, and last fifty years as well as one. We stopped an hour. The gentlemen bought cigars, and the ladies bought apricots of the natives, and olive-cheeked boys came aboard and sang plaintive little airs to words we could not understand, except "Savoy, Savoy," keeping time with a poor old rack-o'-bones guitar. They looked like pictures of *improvvisatores*, and had a most poetic appearance, in spite of dirt. I could not help noticing that each one wore a seal-ring.

Yes, that was Ajaccio, and I had lived to see with my own eyes the halcyon waves breaking on the serene shore. If the boy be, indeed, father of the man, the young Bonaparte must have dreamed, like Joseph among his brethren in the field of Shechem, that their sheaves bowed obedience to his, that their stars paled before his own. On this playground he must have known himself superior to his narrow island home and kindred, but could not have thought himself a centre round which they should cluster, an emperor making kings at a word and distributing crowns like ribbons and badges.

The fourth person in our party is the Antiquary, who has lately written an exhaustive work (to the reader) on the Prehistoric Man. He wore green goggles at sea, to guard his eyes, which are always red; at their corners the blackest bird that flies has set his footprints, and digging Greek roots is not calculated to clear them of wrinkle or color. He stood with us on deck, watching the grouping in the pretty town. "Now," he said, with the air of a man firing a bomb, "we are near the land of one of the most depraved men that ever breathed the breath of life."

The missile struck as he had foreseen.

"He was a hero, and I glory in him," retorted Thalia, with the freshness of unworn enthusiasm.

"You glory in one who would never glory in you or any daughter of Eve," said Antiquary, severely and aggressively. "Women were merely a means of population to him; and when he used to ask, apropos of nothing, 'Madame, how many sons have you?' he was only thinking how many conscripts she could furnish for his thinning ranks. With all his genius, he never was a gentleman. Men were knives to him, women the forks, and with them he carved the world up."

"How savage you are!" said Thalia, tartly. "You know they always loved him."

"Yes, he was magnetic; he drew them by some unknown attraction, -- a secret power of great men. It was partly his appearance. Like Alcibiades, he was beautiful at every age. The French portraits of him, from Italy to Moscow, are perfect pictures, and the bust made during the campaign in Egypt, the property of the late Mrs. Susan Bonaparte, of Baltimore, is the most exquisite thing I ever saw in marble. It might well stand for an ideal head of Poetry, Apollo, Morning, and is entirely without the heaviness of the later portraits. Even the dying figure, by Nèle, is more beautiful in death than any other in perfect health."

"How about Josephine?" asked Thalia, with a slight sneer on her pretty lips.

"Oh! she was a soft, cat-like Creole, pliant as oil, who knew how to yield gracefully where she could not control. The woman twice married, who would have been twice divorced but for the death of Beauharnais, is not such as you love." And he bowed his antiquated bow.

"She loved him to the last."

"Yes, selfishness never fails to find its worshippers, -- in Dickens, for instance. The Bonapartes were absorbents. The world was created for them, and they divided it among themselves."

The Antiquary is an elderly, not to say old, bachelor, usually mild and softly spoken, now a little warmed over his subject. He took off the goggles, breathed on them, and polished them by rubbing with a scrap of chamois, kept for the purpose in his watch-pocket.

"Napoleon should have died at Waterloo," he continued. "You know he practised *pose* and drapery under Talma, and, with his sharp eye for dramatic effect, should have seen the grand theatric stroke in leading the Old Guard in a dying charge; but no. He poetically writes: 'Since it is not permitted me to die in the field,' etc. Had he dashed into the thick of the fight that last day, I do believe Fate would have accepted his death. What a glamour and daze there was in the name of Napoleon forty years ago! Happily it is being blown away. Humbug! humbug! The French are always after striking effects."

"And lovely ones they make," said Thalia, warmly.

"You remember," said the scoffer, without heeding the interruption, "Danton's dying words to Samson, the headsman: 'Thou wilt show my head to the people. It is worth showing.' And Mirabeau, rousing from the dulness of death at the sound of cannon: 'What, have we the Achilles's funeral already?' modestly alluding to self. Those Revolutionists always managed to appear near the footlights at the front of the stage, and strike a fine attitude as the curtain fell to slow music. How much claptrap there is in Paris -- France, to be sure, to be sure!"

Thalia turned away, and took up her Ollendorf, applying herself to the study of that ridiculous guide, philosopher, and friend of youth who teaches language in wise questions and answers: "Does the good Russian wish to buy the fine looking-glass of the tailor's boy; or that of the sailors with the silver candlestick and pretty umbrellas?" etc.

I heard the steady buzz, buzz; but knew it would not last long, for Thalia hates study. This was only a pretence. She was vexed, and a blood-spot glowed in each cheek, -- "a rose in the snow." Presently she laid down the book, and, looking over the guard into the bright, transparent water, she asked: "What do you suppose would have happened had Bonaparte conquered the Continent, as he hoped to do?"

"He would have made Rome the centre, the poor little Duke of Reichstadt his king and successor, and would have lorded it like the latter-day emperors of Rome. Possibly, to amuse the people, he might have ordered the old soldiers to be given to the lions of the circus, as they used to be thrown away, because fighting-men worn out are useless, and after exhausting wars meat is dear. He was none too good for that. Men were, in his estimate, only cannon-balls, -- useful implements of war."

"There must have been good in him," said Thalia, excitedly, "We never had a general whose six brigadiers would follow him to exile in an island where no one, foreign or native, was ever known to live sixty years." And here she took a scrap from the guide-book and read: "All wept, but particularly Savary and a Polish officer, who had been exalted from the ranks by Bonaparte. He clung to his master's knees; wrote a letter to Lord Keith entreating permission to accompany him, even in the most menial capacity, --

'ALL I ASK IS TO DIVIDE
EVERY PERIL HE MUST BRAVE,
SHARING, BY THE HERO'S SIDE,
HIS FALL, HIS EXILE, AND HIS GRAVE.'"

14

"Good, if true," said Antiquary, dryly. "It sounds mightily like French clap-trap."

"You are incorrigible, and I close this talk with an appeal to the silent woman."

"This is not my funeral, Thalia, and I save my tears for fresher graves."

Antiquary walked to the prow, to watch the dolphins play, and Thalia picked up her Afghan stripe again. She is a true golden blonde. You do not see four such heads in a lifetime. But little past her first youth, not over twenty-eight; the gold of her hair still untarnished; her eyes blue as wild violets, without a dash of gray or brown; clear pink and white skin; little teeth, white as milk, in a dimpled baby mouth, -- such is my Thalia; the widow of a rich, but honest commission merchant of Chicago, lovely in her mourning draperies as she never had been in her day of blue ribbons, and not unlike the portrait of Lady Hamilton, beloved of Nelson, which hangs in the National Gallery, London. A woman feminine in every fibre, body and soul, who had kept her pure childish beliefs, her cradle faith in men and God, to mature years; one to be adored because she herself was a worshipper, and the most lovable person I have known, taking her for all in all. She had her tempers, however, as you will discover when you "get acquainted," as we journey on.

"Willy always believed in Napoleon," she said softly, as to herself.

And who was Willy? Her husband of seven months, -- killed, crushed under a grain elevator. In life, she had called him "Will," but a new tenderness came to her voice when that mangled corpse was brought home and she laid the pathetic clay in the dust toward which it was drawn by such mysterious kinship.

Reclining in her easy-chair, the light, fluffy hair against the black shawl, Thalia was very fair to see, and I watched the blue eyes grow dreamy and moist while she was busy with memory. They were with her heart, and that was far away. Willy Benson's outer life was an every-day story. Emphatically a working-man, his subordinates called him a little hard, but the home side of his heart was warm as June. Whatever business troubles he had he bore alone. The heat and dust of the warehouse were not for her; the rain must not dampen her feet nor the winds of heaven visit her too roughly. His calm, earnest way of loving had won her whole soul; but not at first sight, for she was another Portia, --

"HER SUNNY LOCKS
HANG ON HER TEMPLES LIKE A GOLDEN FLEECE,
AND MANY JASONS COME IN QUEST OF HER."

She loved him with the love which comes but once in a lifetime, and her seven months of marriage were the seven golden sheaves in the vision of the patriarch, the seven shining lamps in the most holy place.

Oh, blessed, transfiguring light, which falls like the light which fell but once on Tabor! Be their earthly lives what they may, when the beloved pass beyond the veil, every earthly fault is dropped with the outworn earthly garment, and from out the shining cloud their far-reaching voices come back, like the voices of those who have learned of the angels.

III. AMONG THE BRIGANDS

AJACCIO used to be a great place for brigands," I said, as we pushed out to sea.

"They are pretty well rid of about this place," said Antiquary, with the positive air of one who knows, "and the outlaws of the Mediterranean are now in force, organized and equipped, in Asia Minor. When I was here, ten years ago, I heard a story and read a paper, duly attested and sworn to by a British subject, whose name you doubtless saw in the New York papers of the time."

"Let us have the story," said Thalia, delightedly. "I know it is just like 'Irving's Sketch Book,'--three robbers, with belts full of pistols, and red sashes, spring out of a thicket; the traveller is throttled, gagged, carried up the mountain side and--"

"I thought I was to be the story-teller. Pardon the interruption; but you allow imagination to run away with you."

"True, O king! But make it long and make it romantic. On ship there is so much time, time, time!" She tapped the deck with the toe of her little boot and waited attentively.

"I am sorry not to do that," said the Antiquary; "but, in touching a record witnessed and sworn to, I must tell the tale as 'twas told to me. The hero was no longer young, and quite bald," he continued, with an ironic smile and the particularizing way of one who writes more than he talks and is used to good listeners. "His name was Johnson, and he had a farm about the size of Cincinnatus's, where the plough has been standing in the midst of the furrow many centuries. You may have had some remote hint of that ancient agricultural implement in your school days. It was not a great way from Sorrento. One winter night -- "

"I thought it was always summer in Italy," struck in Thalia.

"They have wretched, raw days there, when the orange-trees shiver with snow and the mountain air is frosty and biting. Let me get on with my yarn, or the *garçon* will clear the decks before I am done. This was a cold, snowy night. Mr. Johnson was warm in his comfortable library, when he was startled by shots rattling against the iron shutters and blows against the door below. The house was of brick; the lower floor a granary, which had no interior communication with the rest of the rooms. Mrs. Johnson hid in her boudoir, and Mr. Johnson went upon the roof and fired in the direction of the sound and flashes of light. The brigands were under cover. He wounded a few boards in the outhouse; but nothing else was hurt. Presently there was a crash below, and smoke, bursting from the lower windows, announced the robbers had got in and were setting fire to the house. Nothing was left the gallant Englishman (did I tell you this was a British subject?) but to come down and surrender. He knew he would not be harmed, nor would his wife; for all the brigands want is the ransom which they have learned by experience England is ready to advance for the lives of her officers. Mr. Johnson found the lower floor in possession of the gang, who saluted him with politeness and assured him they had no intention of frightening any one. The chief ordered the trembling servants to put out the fire of lighted straw, which had been kindled on the stone floor and did no damage. They had left the forest, which is their haunt, shortly after dark, sent their servant in advance with meat to silence the watch-dogs, and so won an easy victory.

"At the door was Mr. Johnson's own riding-horse, saddled and bridled, and his wife's brown mare waiting. The robber explained that he took only the dark horses and had left the gray in the stable because its color would show in the starlight. He then ordered Mr. Johnson to go upstairs and bring *Miladi*, which was done. Before mounting her horse, for whom the chief held the stirrup, Mrs. Johnson asked leave to collect a few trifles necessary for a lady's comfort on a short journey, giving her *parole d'honneur* she would make no signal, noise, or outcry. There was no one to see if she did. The gallant outlaw gave permission, and her valise of valuables was taken in charge by the chief. As they afterward learned, the robbers were seven in number, -- four Algerines, three Greeks, one formerly a monk at Mount Athos. Strange to tell, he still wore his old monastic habit and made the sign of the cross before and after meals. From the beginning, the Greeks have been a nation of pirates, by sea and by land. The ancient heroes were merely organized corsairs, ready to fight each other, as they were the enemy in the plains of Troy. Ajax was forever in a pout, sulking about the camp; and Achilles threatening to sail off with his command, back to Greece. But this is getting ahead of my story.

"The troops surrounded the prisoners by order of the chief, Leonidas (the glorious old names have never dropped out of Grecian memory), struck into a sharp pace, and, after two hours of absolute silence in the rugged road, the lady complained of fatigue. The band halted in a ruined tower, of Venetian work, and held a whispered council. After lively disputes under their breath (for the Greeks are nothing if not wordy), Leonidas announced to Mrs. Johnson that she was *impedimenta* -- too great an incumbrance for them to carry -- and must return home. She must tell no one what had happened for two days (the servants had already been warned), and at the end of that time she should see the British authorities, and speedily arrange a ransom. 'Else,' said the brigand, with an ominous gesture across his throat, 'it will go hard with our captive.'

"'And must I ride back through this awful road alone?' asked the timid lady.

"'By no means,' rejoined the polite outlaw. 'Brother Basil will escort you.'

"'And may I say good-by to my husband before I leave him, maybe forever?' she asked, bursting into tears.

"'It can do no harm; but be quick and be still about it. I hate a crying woman. She unsettles everything.'"

"It is all like a romance," said the pleased, intent Thalia.

"Yes, Italy *is* a story-book. The very stones in the streets are over-written with them. This is no romance; a plain, unvarnished tale under oath, a deposition.

"The lady was conducted home in peace and safety, and Brother Basil refreshed himself with wine, bread, and grapes before starting back to rejoin his comrades.

"In the gray of the morning the gang, with Mr. Johnson, entered a cave, kindled a little fire, cooked a kid, and made coffee. Then the whole party slept, except one sentinel, relieved every two hours.

"About noon the chief dictated a letter to the British authorities at Rome. If the ransom was not forthcoming in ten days, the ears of the prisoner would be sent in; if not in eight, his nose; if not in ten, his head. Besides the ransom demanded, eight thousand pounds sterling, there must be two gold watches, with chains, three amber cigar-holders, and four breechloading revolvers, silver-mounted, and of superior make and finish. If pursued, the prisoner would be killed instantly. The obedient captive wrote the letter on the little pine table which served for the dinner. It was scanned with the utmost care by Leonidas, and then sent off by a peasant, summoned by a sailor's whistle from the forest. The prisoner was then blindfolded, and again the mounted gang pressed up a rocky path, very steep, as Johnson knew by the motion of the horse. They halted by day and rode by night, two days and nights. Then a second letter was dictated. The chief had neglected to mention in the former letter that if there was any bad money in the bags the sum demanded for their captive's ransom would be doubled.

"The final halt was made in a great cavern, under a hill, used as a storehouse by the robbers, where all sorts of spoil had accumulated. There was a bed of good mattresses for the tired prisoner, and the men received guests and made merry with wine and wassail, in which Brother Basil gayly held his own, as the bottle went merrily round."

"Did they treat poor Mr. Johnson cruelly?"

"Not at all. Their interest was to keep him alive and well; a dead man has no money value among thieves. The chief remarked, in explanation of their scant fare, that gentlemen of his profession were hard up, the government officials had grown so vigilant. However, the prisoner always had his plenty of bread, goat's flesh, and wine, when the outlaws were on half rations. He gradually grew into a sort of companionship with the reformed monk."

"Reformed! When, I pray to know."

"Entirely reformed," said Antiquary, pleased with the feeble joke, "and he was a capital hand at cards and the Roman game mora. The ten days went by, twelve, twenty, still no friendly messenger from the home authorities; no white flag, nor peasant bearing despatches with official seal. Then a third letter was dictated. If the ransom was not paid over at a certain time and place, the captive would be flayed alive, or, as they put it, make a jacket *a la Franca*; that is, the skin of the upper part of the body would be removed, and the martyred Johnson roasted *a la broche*. He now began to be seriously alarmed. He had assurance that active and powerful friends were busy; but there might be some hitch in the proceedings and he be killed. Besides, the gang began to be quarrelsome, and some of their brawls were well-nigh fatal. As a rule, divisions of spoils were made in absolute submission to the chief; but one dispute warmed into a fight, in which blows were freely exchanged. It was over the disposal of lockets, ladies' rings, and a superb watch, set with diamonds. This last was the special admiration of Brother Basil.

"The weather was bitter cold, and the wind swept into the cavern, where fire was rarely lighted by day, unless in foggy or snowy weather. The horses fared badly, without shelter and a meagre allowance of hay. One day another prisoner was brought in by the Algerines, badly wounded and with one arm broken. He begged hard for life, only life on any terms, and Johnson added his entreaties; but the man was shot and hastily buried in a shallow pit."

"Poor fellow!" said the soft-hearted Thalia, pityingly.

"He was much the same stripe as his captors: all thieving cutthroats. I have seen these fellows often about Smyrna and Rhodes. They are handsome rascals, with keen, luminous eyes, hair and beard so black as at first to give the impression of being dyed, so utterly without shading is it. Each one has his curious ring, worn for some superstition (I do not know what), and a quiet, observant way of watching, without seeming to see anything, from under those jetty eyebrows, which often meet across the forehead. But this is a digression, as our friends the novelists say.

"Every day, at noon, the brigands had intelligence of some sort. They knew well what was going on in the cities, and the peasants of Italy knew some illustrious prisoner was being held for ransom. Any information given by them to the Government spies and officials would be paid for with the loss of all they had, if not of their heads. Johnson had the great relief of hearing the sailor's whistle several times a day, and gathered that his friends were stirring and thoroughly in earnest. Scouts came in often, and, from the bustle and debates in camp, he felt sure his captivity was well-nigh ended.

"At last, the happy day came. The robbers, with their captive, met a delegation of three Englishmen at an appointed place in the forest. The bags of money were unloaded from a mule; opened; each piece counted and inspected, to see there was no spurious coin and no marks to give a clew to their whereabouts afterward.

"The watches and amber cigar-holders were not forgotten in the exchange, and a Martini rifle was offered and rejected.

"Leonidas wanted a Winchester 'with many cartridges.' What a contrast these well-mounted, well-armed bands are with the ragamuffins of fifty years ago, who had nothing but blunderbusses and dagger!

"After some grumbling and much swearing, the prisoner was delivered up to his friends. While the money was being counted, they had shaved him, cut his unkempt hair, and given him a good breakfast of broiled kid and white bread. Then Brother Basil graciously spread his fat hand above Johnson's uneasy head and gave him his blessing, shook hands with him, and, in flattering terms, expressed his happiness at having so long enjoyed the society of such a distinguished prisoner, -- one worth ten thousand pounds to his country; yes, and more too.

"The brigands returned six Napoleons, borrowed of Johnson in the cave, and a revolver. They also gave him the worst horse in their forest stable, and the captive of three months rode away with his friends a sadder and a wiser man."

"There is a sort of unreality about this story," I said.

"I grant it," said Antiquary; "but if you will read the newspapers of the Levant, you will see there is not the least exaggeration, and that the British Government has served notice on the brigands of all nationalities that no more ransoms will be paid."

"A romantic tale."

"Yes; but strictly true. I should have mentioned that the robbers brought frequent letters from Mrs. Johnson to her husband, and he was allowed to write open letters to her, which Leonidas gave to Brother Basil, as the best scholar of the gang, to see if there was no concealed writing or marks conveying secret intelligence. They never ate meat on Fridays, were deeply superstitious, and trembled and dropped on their knees at the sound of thunder."

"Why do not the peasants inform on them?"

"As I told you, through fear of their own fields and cottages. When the season is good, the brigands make presents to the poorest, and one has been known to pay the expense of educating the eldest son of one of his humble admirers; for the lower classes have the deepest admiration of all this bravado, and the desperadoes are welcome in hut and bower to the *contadina*. Many a time I've seen them in the dance with the pretty peasant girls, and the most noted are in high favor with the simple creatures, given to hero worship. Women are given to adoration the world over, you know, and themselves create the *aura* of the divinity before whom they kneel."

IV. IN AND ABOUT TUNIS

I KNOW nothing more disappointing than an olive grove. Its feathery, silver-gray foliage has been described in many books, and its associations with Gethsemane and Calvary have given it a sacredness which prepared me to salute it with becoming reverence. An old chronicler writes that the tablet of the title above our Saviour's cross they made of olive because it betokens peace, "and the story of Noah witnesseth that the dove brought the branch of olive, and it betokened peace made between God and man; and so the Jews expected to have peace when Christ was dead, for they said he made discord and strife among them."

These exquisite lines of Ruskin had hung it with poetry as a halo and a glory: --

"I challenge the untravelled English reader to tell me what an olive-tree is like. I know he cannot answer my challenge. He has no more idea of an olive-tree than if olive-trees grew only in the fixed stars. Let him meditate a little on this one fact and consider its strangeness, and what a wilful and

constant closing of the eyes to the most important truths it indicates on the part of the modern artist. Observe a want of perception, not of science. I don't want painters to tell me any scientific facts about olive-trees; but it had been well for them to have felt and seen the olive-tree; to have loved it for Christ's sake, partly also for the helmed Wisdom's sake, which was to the heathen in some sort as that nobler Wisdom which stood at God's right hand when he founded the earth and established the heavens. To have loved it even to the hoary dimness of its delicate foliage, subdued and faint of line, as if the ashes of the Gethsemane agony had been cast upon it forever, and to have traced, line for line, the gnarled writhings of its intricate branches and the pointed fretwork of its light and narrow leaves inlaid on the blue field of the sky, and the small rosy white stars of its spring blossoming, and the beads of sable fruit scattered by autumn along its topmost boughs, the right in Israel of the stranger, the fatherless, and the widow, and, more than all, the softness of the mantle, silver gray and tender, like the down on a bird's breast, with which, far away, it veils the undulation of the mountains, -- these it had been well for them to have seen and drawn, whatever they had left unstudied in the gallery."

I saw scraggy, famished specimens in Southern France, and said to myself: "It is too far west for them here. I must wait till we reach the Orient, and then I will see them, lush and juicy, full of the familiar *huile d'olive* associated with salads the world over." They are a low-limbed, stunted race, gnarled and twisted in growth; so scrubby and rusty as to give the same impression that scant fare and hard living give to the pinched faces of a stunted race of men, -- say the Irish peasants. The first close acquaintance I had with them was in North Africa, and I felt imposed on, that such low-lived bushes had been held up by poets and saints, who ought to have had the truth before their eyes, as forming rich and shady arcades of delicate leafage. They were the genuine olive green, however, -- the dull, dark shade fashionable among ladies who affect charming selections of color; and the subdued bronze green casts a sombre, dusky shadow. But do not call those haggard, meagre, wrinkled shrubs trees in the hearing of a Western woman, used to the forest kings of the Mississippi Valley, -- the grand old beeches, with hoary trunks, immovable against wind and storm as columns of sculptured stone; the oaks, dewy and fresh at noon, their far-reaching branches, like patriarchal hands, extended in blessing.

Tunis is not, as I had fancied it, built on the site of ancient Carthage, but fully two hours' ride distant. I had a fond dream there of riding on swift Arab steeds, shod with fire, such as sweep with flying mane and tail through Oriental song and romance; but we were obliged to content ourselves with the scriptural ass. In the cool of the morning (not that it was cool), we set out, a merry party of four, on donkeys, each with its attendant runner, who poked the wretched creatures with sticks sharpened for the purpose. The donkey gait is racking and tiresome, a forlorn contrast to the anticipated Arabians, gentle as a woman, easy as a cradle, fleet as the wind; but, then, what is experience but another name for disappointment? The sun made glorious a clear cut rocky range which bounds the horizon; and the bare, craggy Jebel Rasas, or mountain of lead, did its best to look bright and precious in the keen white light. It is the boldest point in the Tunisian landscape which catches the eye and holds it above the dull, widespread monotony of color below. The name is not a misnomer, for it was worked by the Carthaginians two thousand years ago, and afterward by the Romans; and a few Arabs, in dingy turbans, still picking and pretending to work at the dark chambers in the mountain-side.

We left the walled city and passed unchallenged the unkempt, ununiformed soldiers which constitute the Bey's defenders, and were at once in the open country, which had the peculiarity of being destitute of roads, except one to the Bey's Palace of the Bardo, about three miles off. We ambled slowly along a bridle-path, through the disappointing olive orchards, coated with dust, moving Indian file and in Indian silence, for the excursion was proving wofully unlike our anticipations. Venerable aloe-trees, with their gigantic flower-stems, fenced in worn-out patches of ground, poorly cultivated, yet showing the pomegranate, with its fruit a glowing scarlet ball, and purple figs, which should be more delicious than they are, they look so luscious and inviting. Our rough path of uneven clay at intervals brought us near the Mediterranean bank; and the clear, exquisite tint of the sparkling sea enchanted the sight with its restful blue. As the day advanced, the sand-hills were like heaps of heated burnished metal, and we all wished we had provided ourselves with thick veils, or, better still, antiquarian goggles. Gradually the poor huts and poorer gardens disappeared, and we entered an open, dreary, empty plain, marked by what might be called a single trail. Our guide rode on ahead, and, while we were trying to recall and make useful chapter and verse of the Punic wars, he waved his hand, the vivacious Greek, and shouted, "Carthago." The boys whipped up the bony donkeys; we reached Aristides, who stood with head uncovered while we looked about us. There was no column, base, or capital, no arch or cornice, frieze or foundation stone. As the children say, there was "no nothing." Well has Cato's menace been fulfilled: *Delenda est Carthago*. We had the sensation of one who has run to a fire and found it put out before his arrival. The ground was irregular and broken with depressions here and there, but no ruins of the great city that for a hundred years rivalled Rome, and with her disputed supremacy of the seas from the islands of the Hellespont to the Pillars of Hercules. Corners of brickwork pushed out through the poor soil, spotted with splashes of crumbling plaster, not of Dido's city, but vestiges of the Roman Carthage built by Caesar and Augustus and made the capital of Africa. It was destroyed in 698 by the Arabs and left not a wrack behind.

"Let us have a fire and make a cup of tea, that there may be something in the place where Carthage is not," said our leader.

"The best thought advanced yet," said Thalia. "But where shall we find a cooling shadow in this weary land?"

We looked about. There was no rock, no wall, no hill nor mound high enough to cast a shade; no tree, not even a despised olive or famished fig, which lives on starvation. Our well-kept raptures were not to be expended on the site of the haughty city, and we tamely followed the guide into a cavernous hole, with vaulted roof, the remains of the antique cisterns of Carthage, where robbers burrow in winter. The Bedouins had left ashes of old fires in tiny heaps on the floor, and the arch above was smoky, showing long use. There was nothing to dispute possession of the den, and one runaway scorpion was the sole tenant. An Arab boy, with lean and hungry look, who had hung round us all the way from Tunis, now appeared, holding a few twigs of brushwood, which he fanned into a cheerful blaze with a scrap of palm-leaf; and, really, the sight of flame and smell of smoke were the most welcome sight we had in this classic spot. The fifth donkey, a scraggy little beast, about the size of a

Newfoundland dog, was brought; a Persian rug was unloaded from his back; various cans, boxes, and packages, and the tea-caddy (which the traveller in the East soon learns to love) were strewed over the floor. That was a new experience, picnicking in the water-tanks of Carthage; and eggs, sardines, bread, grapes, and sweet oranges made a feast fit for the king. I doubt if our predecessors ever enjoyed a noonday lunch half so much. Overhead was a hillock rising above the subterranean arch, perhaps twenty feet from the empty level. On it or near it must have stood Hannibal, Marius, Scipio, in the dim old historic years, when the bare blank country was a crowded city in the midst of the garden and granary, the rich corn-lands of Africa. Here it was the lamenting Dido invoked the three hundred gods, and said to Sister Anna she was tired of the azure heaven above. Here

"BENEATH THE SKY
A LOFTY PILE BEING BUILT, OF TARRY PINE
AND ILEX SPLIT, THE QUEEN HANGS GARLANDS ROUND,
AND CROWNS THE PYRE WITH FUNERAL LEAVES, AND LAYS
THEREON THE ROBES AND SWORD; AND ON THE COUCH
HIS EFFIGY; WELL KNOWING WHAT WOULD COME."

Unhappy queen! Aeneas was not worth her tears even: but she gave him her life. It is comforting to know she never existed, she who appears more real to the traveller than the conquerors who followed each other like dim phantoms of the past.

Said Antiquary, speaking as one having authority: "The latter-day luxury and riot of Rome came from the East. Gladiators had no part in her exhibitions till the Punic wars, and, though the Imperial City overturned Carthage and Corinth, it was greatly influenced by them both. The Carthaginians were from Tyre, the Shemitic race. They were dreadful idolaters. Moloch was one of their chief gods."

"The Sunday-school Moloch?" asked Thalia.

"The same," replied Antiquary, with a wrinkled smile, which made him look like the dried-apple dolls on sale at country church festivals. "A brass statue, with hollow body, fire inside. The arms, red-hot, received the child, who struggled and fell into the coals beneath the base. Sometimes, when battles failed, the generals did not scruple to offer prisoners, and even their own soldiers, in sacrifice to the terrible deity."

They deserved destruction," I said.

"Yes; they were always faithless and treacherous. The army was an army of mercenaries; the seamen, slaves chained to the oars, who never left the galleys. Their generals valued men as ours do perfect machinery. The old battles must have been murderous, for after the battle of Cannae three bushels of rings were taken from the frozen fingers of Roman knights and sent by Hannibal home to Carthage."

Thalia reclined on the Persian rug at ease, resting her back against a loose pile of brick-work, and we disposed ourselves comfortably as we might in the broken cistern which sheltered from the noonday sun. "It is too hot to go out yet. Tell me some story about this place," said the beauty; "my mother tried to hire me to read Rollin, but I never got beyond Egypt."

"The best thing that can be told of all that time is the story of Regulus. 'Tis an old tale and often told, but never worn out. There was no man in this dead city fit to loose the latchet of his shoes, and such was the stern old Roman virtue that the most constant of Rome's enemies trusted the most unrelenting of her officers with a boundless faith. Such men are of those who are born to rule the world; from the beginning elected to the divine right, crowned and anointed at their birth.

V. A DAY IN CARTHAGE

"BUT about Regulus," said Antiquary, walking up and down the narrow cistern cave. "In the fifth year of his captivity an embassy from Carthage was sent to Rome, and he accompanied the ambassadors, under promise to return to his prison if the proposals offered were declined. Many an orator has spoken, and many a poet harped and sung, how, when he reached his own city, he at first refused to enter it, because he was the slave of the Carthaginians. When brought before the Senate, which received him with the honors he had never failed to deserve, he declined to give an opinion, as he had ceased by his captivity to be a member of that illustrious body, being degraded to the level of a slave. At length, when persuaded by his countrymen to speak, he implored the Senate to acknowledge no peace, and to decline even an exchange of prisoners. When he saw them wavering from their desire to redeem him from captivity, he said the enemy had given him slow poison, which soon would send him unto the silent majority. And at last, when the Senate, through his pleadings, refused the offered terms of the Carthaginians, he resisted the prayers of his friends to remain in Rome, false to his word, and returned to

Carthage, where a martyr's death awaited him. It is told he was placed in a barrel lined with spikes of iron, and was rolled over and over till he perished. Others say that his eyelids were cut off, and he was then thrown into a dark dungeon, from which he was suddenly brought out and exposed to the full rays of a burning sun. It is not clearly known, -- only that he made himself a place among the immortal names.

"The Roman spirit is dead here. It went out with the republic; but it still lives in our own country. If President Lincoln had been kidnapped, as was at first intended by the rebels, I do believe he would not have counted his life dear unto himself could it have been weighed against the safety of the republic. He, too, would have implored the Senate to submit to no ignoble terms, and would have gone back to the black bread and carrion of Andersonville, sharing its slow poison with the lowest soldier, dying in unspeakable filth and misery, rather than treat with rebels. The heroism of the high Roman was not nobler than that of the plain man of our prosaic age, in homely guise, working out the grand results to which he was ordained. But he is too near our eyes for the lights of airy and remote distance; and no color of fable tinges the name and fame of the man who led us in stormy times, -- the shepherd of his people."

After a pause he resumed: --

"They were stout fighters, those old Carthaginians. In the last siege of the city, vessels of silver and gold were given for arms, and possession was battled from street to street with the energy of despair. Dead bodies were used for ramparts; the fire lasted seventeen days; and even Scipio was moved to tears at the utter wretchedness of the powerful city.

"On the very hillock above us, perhaps, he repeated the words of the Iliad over the flames: 'The day shall come when sacred Troy shall perish, and Priam and his people shall be slain.'

"It was here the women gave their hair for bowstrings. Thalia's rich, silky locks would have made a very Cupid's bow for a swift-flying arrow."

I looked at her, and she was fast asleep. The third Punic war is altogether too much for the woman who does not like study. We forgive everything to beauty; and the delicate, girlish shape, made of the refined clay of which Nature is most sparing, rested against the Persian rug like the pictures of the gentle Mohammedan Peris, who subsist on perfumes, mainly musk. No one disturbed her siesta or resented the slight; and while I watched her the gentlemen rambled out in search of a white stone with which to mark the day, but failed to find one worth stooping to pick up. The temples, amphitheatres, forums, have passed from sight; nothing remains but the storied sea and the proud harbor, where the countless fleets lay anchored. All, all gone, the grandeur and the glory!

My reader who visited the Centennial may remember, in the Tunisian Department, an ancient mosaic from the floor of a Carthaginian palace. The design was a lion, and the make rude and uneven. Maybe the wearing centuries had rubbed away some of its polish; but I am free to maintain that specimen of Carthaginian art was a damaging blow to my early notions of the pristine splendors of the Orient. Still, good judges professed to believe it was an admirable work. You, my beloved, must make your own choice. All beauty is in the eye of the gazer, and no one can judge for another.

Long after the Phoenician Carthage had been swept away, after the Roman city ceased to exist, after the Vandal and the Arab, came here armies, gorgeous, magnificent, upholding the emblem of peace for the most merciless of wars. In 1248 St. Louis of France and his three brothers received from the Abbey of St. Denis the pilgrim's scrip and staff and the sacred oriflamme, delegated to him by the holy men who were forbidden to use arms personally, to be borne before the abbot in battle. The king sailed, with his barons and vassals, haughty and defiant, and arrived in Cyprus with fifty thousand men, bearing banners that "bloomed with crimson," resplendent with jewels and gold. Each feudal baron had the right to his own standard in the field; and in the rosy island, sacred to Love and Beauty, the mailed armor of the knights, made of glittering rings, gave back the mildly tempered sunlight of that soft region of poetry and romance. All that skill could devise in the way of ornamentation of shield, sword, lance, was wrought into the arms of the later Crusaders. Gunpowder has blown away much of the pomp and circumstance of glorious war; and historians unite in testimony that a more gallant army never took the field than that which went out on the eighth Crusade.

Egypt was the object of Louis's first attack, the deliverance of Palestine being hoped from the conquest of the land of Mizraim. A storm dispersed his fleet soon after leaving Cyprus; and the royal division, in which were nearly three thousand knights and their following, arrived off Damietta before the rest appeared. The shores were lined with the Sultan's troops. The unearthly din of their horns and kettledrums struck the French with dismay; and the splendor of their arms of barbaric gold was so brilliant, that "when the sun shone on the commander, he seemed like the sun itself." The counsellors urged Louis to wait for the rest of his army; but the pious and intrepid monarch waited not for his impatient knights, tossing on the stormy sea. Harnessed in complete armor, a shining shield pendent from his neck, lance in hand, and the consecrated oriflamme borne before him, he leaped the waves breast high, among the foremost who reached the shore. The Mussulmans fled in panic, and the French quietly took possession of Damietta: but the enemy rallied and returned in great numbers, and, after a bloody struggle, the French were routed. The king, separated from the rest of the army, was captured, with the whole of his nobles, and ransomed with ten thousand golden bezants. Thus closed the eighth Crusade, in bitter lamenting that the very bloom and flower of chivalry had been sacrificed in vain.

The appalling situation of Christian forces in Asia Minor determined King Louis to put his fortunes to the touch in a final enterprise. He summoned his barons and knights, some of whom cursed his folly, and refused to join him. He and his three sons then put on the cross for the last time. He was old and gray; but his faith was clear, and his unbending will had not begun to waver. His host was numerous, and his plan was first to subdue the Moslems of North Africa. Accordingly, he encamped near Tunis; and his camp was vari-colored, radiant with hundreds of banners floating on the warm winds. Every sort of arm, device, and ensign fluttered softly in the breeze, that blew now from the desert, now from the sea. Instead of victory, there was waiting for him the pestilence which walketh in darkness and wasteth at noonday. Here, on the site of old Carthage, the Christian king added one more renowned name to the still slopes on Fame's eternal camping-ground. He died of malarial fever, August 25, 1270. Many a minstrel and Troubadour of his time sang how Louis, ninth of his name, lay dying on a bed of ashes, the words "Jerusalem! O Jerusalem!" the last on his white lips; and how his weeping knights bewailed him and shrouded him in the lilied flags, the crowned helmet, sword, knightly spurs, and cross-marked shield upon his coffin. For six centuries the grave of the king was neglected, though he was canonized as a saint, and His portrait hung with the most illustrious of the palace galleries of France.

In 1830, the time of Charles X., a treaty was made between France and the Regent of Tunis, containing a special article by which a site for a monument of St. Louis was ceded forever to the King of France; but the kingdom was in revolution, and not till 1841, in the reign of Louis Philippe, was the present memorial chapel raised.

We walked to see it, -- a small, graceful structure of white stone, hardly equal to the monuments that brilliant people usually devote to their beloved dead. The garden in which the chapel stands was doubtless the site of the ancient Byrsa, or Citadel. It contains Roman inscriptions and reliefs of the Imperial Era, found by the French in course of excavation.

The old Crusader sleeps well. Envy and malice no longer whisper that the *motif* of his life was not always above reproach. At this late hour we cannot separate the subtle links which combine good and bad passions, and the human heart is kindly disposed toward the warriors of every grade who battled for the Holy Sepulchre. His errors of deed and judgment are forgiven. What a mixture of romance and nonsense, of splendid achievement and pure folly, is in the dazzling and useless valor of that period!

The Crusades did one good thing for the unborn generations, of which eloquent orators occasionally speak. They have furnished endless debates for ingenuous youth in the land of the free and the home of the brave. Still is the question discussed, and the wrangle contended: Were they or were they not beneficial to mankind? And were Peter and Godfrey, Richard, Raymond, and the rest, of the number of those who had uplifted the human race, when their life-withering marches were closed, "and a mournful and solitary silence prevailed along the coast which had so long resounded with the world's debate"?

That was the golden age of the Troubadours. Poetry was the delight of high and low, and the world was mad with music. With no friend but his harp, the wanderer strolled from town to town, from court to camp, getting supper and bed literally for a song. Every one remembers the sweet story of Blondel and the captive Richard of the Lion Heart, himself a Troubadour. Among the lovers of the gay science were two kings of France, princes, counts, and knights unnumbered. What a contagion the pleasant madness was while the craze lasted! It demanded leisure, enthusiasm, and vivid imagination. Our old earth has grown too cold, too tired, too commonplace for such an epidemic, and now the struggle for bread is too sharp. We have one final hint and dying reminder of those ancient harpers -- Brudder Bones and his merry men, last of the gentle race of Troubadours. Near Carthage, in a lonely spot rarely visited, sleeps a wandering minstrel of our own times, whose one immortal song has been heard wherever the English language is spoken. Like the roving singers of lovely Provence, many times he had nothing but his harp. John Howard Payne was a gay Bohemian, extravagant in taste, lavish in expenditure; living much, too much "'mid pleasures and palaces," yet with a vein of sadness down deep in his heart, an unsatisfied longing for rest never found except in the narrow house appointed for all living. He died while holding the office of consul, and a plain marble slab, sent out by the Government of the United States, marks the grave of the homeless man, sixty years a wanderer on this earth, the author of "Home, Sweet Home."[1]

---

[1] The remains have since been removed to the United States.

One winter he was without money or credit, and in London had not where to lay his head. He tried to quiet the pain of hunger and homelessness by looking in at windows and from the areas scenting good cheer. It was Christmas Eve, the snow fell fast, the wind was sharp and keen. At one luxurious house the hungry man stopped and watched the lighting of the Christmas tree. Its candles streamed brightly on the pavement, and among the evergreens he could see the red berries of holly, the toys and garlands, and the pretty heads of children. They danced and clapped their hands while the presents were distributed, and the air rang with shouts, laughter, and screams of delight. When the merriment had spent itself a little, one young girl went to the piano and struck up "Sweet Home," while the happy family joined in a rousing chorus. Was ever contrast so bitter?

I have this from Mrs. Consul General Heap, on whose head be the blessing of those who entertain strangers. Payne told it to her long after those evil days were passed.

Strolling over the spot where Carthage *is not*, we deeply felt that ours is the continent of Hope and this is the continent of Memory. Here one does not need so much as to stamp his foot to call up ghosts of the past and people space with spirits whose names are a glory which fills the earth. The sun sank behind mysterious hills, a rocky range, with long low outline, marking the limit of the melancholy desert. They were overshadowed by veils (say, rather, a radiance of tinted mists), bright as plumage of birds or hues of flowers; amber, amethyst, and carmine, of unspeakable beauty. Suddenly, out of the fading lights fell violet shadows, such as one never sees in harsher climes. The sea was a sea of glass, mingled with fire.

Grecian peasants say that on the field of Marathon, certain nights, the neighing and trampling of steeds is heard and phantom horse and rider appear in the open plain, "come like shadows, so depart." Thus it was spectral armies marched away with us from the dead city. They were swifter than eagles; they were stronger than lions, -- serried hosts, in the purple and gold of Rome, never breaking, with hoof-beat or steel clash, the spell of that "calmest and most stillest night." Of its exquisite loveliness I hardly trust myself to speak. A tropic air rippled the bay, and, silently donkeying along through the luminous dusk, I thought of the lines a greater than Virgil wrote: --

"IN SUCH A NIGHT
STOOD DIDO, WITH A WILLOW IN HER HAND,
UPON THE WILD SEA-BANKS, AND WAVED HER LOVE
TO COME AGAIN TO CARTHAGE."

The dew of the sea cooled the thirsty land; the moon on the sand lay soft as snow. Under that divine radiance the troubled earth was lulled to rest, hushed as if rocked to sleep by the beating heart in the bosom of the sea. The heavens bent low. Paradise was brought near. The donkey boys ceased their hallooing; solemn silence all, save the low tinkle of a bell where a goat browsed under a famished fig-tree, which had cast its untimely fruit. In the Arab camp a few red coals glowed, a burning spot in the colorless plain.

The weight of old history pressed on my soul with feeling that can never be expressed, -- a sense of the littleness of one petty life in the sight of Him to whom a thousand years are but as yesterday when it is past and as a watch in the night; of the poverty of aims which end with closing breath, of the emptiness of earthly glory beneath the light of the heavenly, I thought, too, and remorsefully, of my own unwritten life, its poor purposes, weak ambitions, grievous mistakes, failures, and looked toward the blue above for comfort. A few stars shone faint and pale through the moon's strong light. In the poetic belief of the Orient they are mystic signs in which the destinies of mortals are written on the everlasting tablet of white pearl extending from east to west, from earth to heaven, and it is guarded by the angels. The decrees of God, the compassionate, are graven there; all fates in the future, all events past, present, and to come, to all eternity. The tired pilgrim looked in vain. To mortal eyes that starry volume is a sealed book. Well are the guardian angels keeping its mighty secrets.

VI. ABOUT THE ARABS

IT was at Tunis I had my first impression of the Arabs; and as Arabia is like no other country, so the Arabs are like no other people. The utter solitude of accursed spots is pictured by this touch; the Arabian shall not pitch his tent there. The wild-eyed Bedouin, unhindered and unharmed, but not harmless, had his beginnings in the land of Shinar, first gathering-place of the sons of men. Irrepressible wanderers, living in strenuous idleness, whose hand is against every man's, of old they broke out of the waterless desert, to raid over Jordan into the green plain of Esdraelon, over the Euphrates, to the civic splendors and rich gardens beyond. From

"THE EASTERN GATE
WHERE THE GREAT SUN BEGINS HIS STATE,"

they now traverse a greater distance than from the Atlantic to the Pacific Ocean. From the Sahara across the land of the Sphinx, and the Phoenix, through which the Nile makes a narrow ribbon of green, they rove and scatter into the great and terrible wilderness where sand-storm rises and simoom blows, and no road ever did or ever will mark its shifting surface. Six hundred miles of land, level as the sea when the wind sleeps, -- well may the poets sing of the endless line of the Sahara and the unsearchable regions of the voiceless, mystic desert. Even here the world does move, and the melancholy silence is no longer broken by the songs of slaves chanting in mournful measure: --

"WHERE ARE WE GOING? WHERE ARE WE GOING?
HEAR US, SAVE US, RUBEE.
MOONS OF MARCHES FROM OUR EYES
BORNOU-LAND BEHIND US LIES;
HOT THE DESERT WIND IS BLOWING,
WILD THE WAVES OF SAND ARE FLOWING;
HEAR US, TELL US, WHERE ARE WE GOING?
WHERE ARE WE GOING, RUBEE?"

Caravans move with the dull, slow, steady tread of camels; but the long files of Ethiop slaves are not in the rear.

The Arab tents are, indeed, black, but comely. As I watched a never-to-be-forgotten sunset, three tents were suddenly pitched, it seemed, against the sky, -- rising swiftly as shapes of genii rise from enchanted depths to startle the sight. Above them four palm-trees, a plumy clump, stood motionless as mirage, every delicate leaf sharp cut against the shining gold. In the farness of the distance a train of overladen camels, slow-moving, winding in serpentine curves across the desert waste, spectral, shadowy, like the pictures of the march of the wise men, every six camels led by a donkey, his driver marching beside him.

The Arabs are the only out-door people I have seen who have beauty of face or grace of movement. The Oriental love of color and floating draperies finds best expression in the white turbans, crimson and green sashes, and floating burnous of the sons of the desert. I do not know if these came from the wilds of the Atlas or the low hills to the east; but, wherever it was, the country was in the limitless realm of poetry, picture, fable, and they were gifted with resistless fascination. A carpet, gay as a peacock's back, was laid in front of the tents. Such were the rugs Haroun al Raschid and his wife, Zobeide, had spread before them all the way when they made the pilgrimage from Bagdad to Mecca. Such was the magic carpet of Hassan, which obeyed his lightest wish and carried him, as on the wings of birds, afloat in the air.

The group upon it was too remote for my seeing; but I could not doubt that among them was a lovely girl, with eyes like the mountain gazelle, and a heart as tameless. Her locks were like midnight, and as a piece of a pomegranate her temples within her locks. She was robed in scarfs and flowing draperies and a gauzy veil, which half concealed her loveliness, according to changeless fashions of the immemorial East. Thus came Rebecca to the well, and she was very fair to look upon, with the wedding gifts on her arms and in her ears, sparkling in the sun's last rays. It sets suddenly here, and darkness falls like a drop-curtain. Under the stars, throbbing white in the indigo blue of that night, was an appeal to fancy such as is never made among Western tribes, whose history, broken and fragmentary, is scarcely worth tracing and knowing. In this new world, which is the old, is limitless suggestion, and at every turn there is kindling for memory and imagination. They were the camping party I watched of the country of Job, greatest of all the men of the East; and of Moses, when he was a stranger and a shepherd. They came from the refuge where Elijah fled for safety, and the murmuring millions of Israel -- the chosen band bearing the coffin of Joseph -- wandered in a pilgrimage such as never was nor never will be made again on earth. With their black bread and dates, coated with a sugary crust, these descendants of Hagar would make their evening meal; and, had we chosen to claim hospitality, doubtless it would have been freely offered as to the stranger in the days of Abraham. The customs of four thousand years are the same. Well has it been said, could Ishmael come again to the earth, he would recognize without effort his own people and his own land.

While these old Bible thoughts went through my mind, suddenly the moving figures stopped, as in the act of listening. We heard nothing but the clumsy stumbling of the mules among the stones. Not a sound but that; yet it was eventide, and somewhere a muezzin was calling to prayer. From the airy top of lofty, remote minarets the faithful had heard a voice we could not hear (*ezan*), calling, in musical, far-reaching wail, the prayer revealed in vision to the Prophet: "God is great! There is no god but God! Mohammed is the prophet of God! Come to prayers! Come to prayers! Prayer is better than sleep!" All the senses of the desert-born are remarkably acute, their eyesight is like clairvoyance, and their hearing appears miraculous. As we lost them in the distance, I could see their prostrations, bowing till their foreheads touched the sand, kneeling and rising again with reverence and devotion. All times and places are alike to them when the hour of worship comes. For the Prophet (exalted be his name!) says: "Every place on earth is given as a place of prayer, except the bath and the grave." I filled up the evening picture, -- the gathering round the tiny fire, where they told the ancient thousand and one stories, forever old, forever new; or the fables of Aesop, called by them Lokman; or the favorite tale, familiar in our schoolbooks, of Llewellyn and his faithful hound, Gelert, which killed the wolf to save his master's child, and was itself killed by the father, when the latter, on entering the hut, saw nothing but an overturned cradle, a pool of blood, and the dog licking his lips.

Their rich and copious language lends itself readily to poetry, and often the stories there would be songs, possibly "very long and very lonesome, and about nothing in particular," or maybe their passionate love of music would have led them to bring along the primitive two-stringed guitar, to accompany the war-song with full chorus, or the soft, grave love ditty to the gazelle-eyed darling in the shadow of the tent. Here is one of the Bedouin songs: --

> "HER SKIN IS LIKE SILK AND HER SPEECH IS LOW, NEITHER REDUNDANT
>   NOR DEFICIENT.
> HER EYES, GOD SAID TO THEM, BE! AND THEY WERE, STIRRING
>   MEN'S HEARTS WITH THE POTENCY OF WINE.
> MAY MY LOVE FOR HER GROW MORE WARM EACH DAY, AND NOT
>   CEASE TILL THE DAY OF JUDGMENT!
> THE LOCKS ON HER BROW ARE DARK AS NIGHT,
> WHILE HER FOREHEAD SHINES LIKE THE GLEAM OF THE
> MORNING.
> AND THE RAIN FALLS NOT, BUT FOR THE PURPOSE OF KISSING THE
>   GROUND BEFORE HER FEET."

Do you recall any line, dear reader, of sweeter exaggeration than that last one? I have heard Arabic music, but the melodies are harsh and irregular, as their verses are smooth and flowing. The lofty imagery of the Orient takes us back to the first love song written to the Egyptian spouse, and the poems of the Arab are filled with spicery, myrrh, and balm, color, and extravagant hyperbole. The scent and soul of the furthest East are in them. They have brave, proud lyrics, full of the spirit of battle, the dust and the rush, the cries and clamor, and are well accompanied by the harsh, tense notes of the zithern. They sing of the ancient fastnesses of their own Arabia, where freemen dwell, in an oasis of freedom, in a world of slaves; and how they drink no wine in a hot and thirsty land, though their wounds consume them, because they have the promise of the Prophet (exalted be his name!) that the faithful shall appear in glory at the resurrection, with their wounds brilliant as vermilion and odoriferous as musk. Led by a beaming light, they will cross the bridge El Sirat, which is fine as the edge of a cimeter, and drink of the Lake of the Happy. It is sweet as honey, cold as snow, clear as crystal. There are streams of milk and of wine, flowing over beds of musk, between margins of camphor, covered with moss and saffron. There they will rest under the wonderful tree of life, Taba, so large that a fleet horse would need a hundred years to cross its shade; and the meanest in Paradise will have seventy-two houris and eighty slaves, eternally young and beautiful forever.

They count a man childless who has only daughters, and around the evening camp-fires they recite a most melancholy tragedy concerning the ancient custom of burying female children alive, practised before the coming of Mohammed, the beloved of God. The tale runs that a chief of Sinai found that among his daughters (who are good for nothing) was one saved alive, and brought up by a neighboring family, unknown to him. She was fair as the moon in her brightness and obedient as the gentle lambs reared in the tents with the women. But the cruel father followed the hideous Proverbs: "To bury daughters is an act of mercy." "An excellent son-in-law is the grave." He watched the chance of carrying her away from her adopted father and mother and heeded not their prayers and entreaties. His heart was hard as the nether millstone. They tell with long, lingering pathos how she hung round her unnatural father's neck, and with terrible minuteness relate how the mother swooned away, but dared not interfere; how, at last, even the flinty nature of the chief was moved, but not far enough to save the child, and the only tears he was ever known to shed were over the little ewe lamb, laid in the living grave, when she reached up and *brushed the grave-dust off his beard!* Heroic songs are the favorites, and old men improvise readily. These reciters, going from camp to camp, as did the Rhapsodists of Greece, keep the unwritten literature of the furthest East; the legends and traditions, which are loaded with imagery; prose and verse, truth and fable, mixed in the strangest way, making rich and exquisite composition. Stories are current of how armies have been stayed and cities saved by the sudden apparition of one of these *Rawis*, with his poetry and his two-stringed guitar, chanting to charmed ears some old tale of woe and wrong, or some wise, measured strain on the changing fortunes of men.

They are not always grave and sober as they appear. The Ishmaelite, the hating man, is not without a dash of humor in his wild blood. Here is one of their tales of a certain Caliph of splendid renown, who died long ago, when the Islam world was young. He had many palaces, with shady fountains ever playing among rings of roses, wild, dark gardens, cooled by rushing waters, running over sands of gold. The Commander of the Faithful had made the holy pilgrimage to Mecca, and kissed the heavenly stone, which was once a pure white jacinth, but has grown black with the kisses of sinful mortals. He had drunk of the sacred well Zemzem, revealed in mercy by the angel to Hagar, and he dwelt in the peace of the blessed. His dishes and goblets were of gold, and his tent, when he journeyed, was a silken pavilion. He had his story-tellers and his dwarfs, dancing girls, and singing women, with musical instruments, and hundreds of slaves, whose lives were in his hand. His heart was warm and at rest. One day he caught a glimpse of a girl with a wandering Bedouin horde. Though dressed in the striped cotton of Yemen, she was like the sun in its brightness and the moon walking among the stars, and from the hour he saw her he neither slept nor ate pleasant bread, for love of her. Vainly did his wise men comfort him, saying the rose from the garden of beauty should be his, if it was predestined, because fifty thousand years before the creation everything was registered in the book of Destiny, and what is not fated can never come to pass. Commit thine affairs unto Him the all-powerful, who spread out the heavens and the earth. The enamored Caliph was a bold believer in the theory that the unchangeable destinies had decreed, preordained, never to be cancelled, his right to the almond-eyed houri in the dress of striped cotton. So he sent officers on steeds shod with fire after the uncle of the girl, who demanded twenty thousand golden dinars for the virgin treasure. It was given without words, and the Caliph thought it all too little for the budding rose, beautiful as the four perfect women with whom Allah has deigned to bless the earth. "The women are all an evil," said Abu Beker, the conqueror; "but the greatest of all evils is that they are necessary." The Damascus palace, with its marble floors and latticed windows, had little charm for her who trod the desert in untrammelled freedom, and whose vision had been bounded by the line where earth and sky meet. The Palace of Delight was only a palace of fears. She pined for the black tents, the long march, the evening bivouac among her homely kindred; and her imperial and imperious husband overheard her singing, half in sorrow, half in scorn, these lines of her own composition: --

"A TENT WHEREIN THE BREEZES FLOW

IS DEARER THAN A PALACE FAIR.
A CRUST UPON THE FLOOR BELOW
    IS CLEARER THAN THE DAINTIEST FARE.
THE WINDS THAT IN EACH CREVICE SIGH
    ARE DEARER THAN THESE DRUMS I HEAR.
AN 'ABBAH' WITH A JOYFUL EYE
    IS DEARER THAN THESE GAUZES HERE.
A DOG THAT BARKS AROUND MY TENT
    IS DEARER THAN A FAWNING CAT.
THE CAMEL FOAL THAT WITH US WENT
    IS DEARER THAN A MULE LIKE THAT.
A BOORISH COUSIN THOUGH HE BE,
    TOO WEAK TO WORK ON MY BEHALF,
WERE DEARER, DEARER FAR TO ME
    THAN YONDER CLUMSY, RAMPANT CALF."

The last couplet enraged the august Caliph, always victorious, and he tore off the Broussa silks and gauzy veil of his unwilling bride, and, giving her the old striped cotton gown and leather slippers, he rained curses on her bare head and sent her back to the desert again. But she went out laughing into the torrid waste, and, when at a safe distance from the Summer Palace, she pulled off the slippers and threw them back, in token of her contempt for the high and mighty Commander of the Faithful, his treasures of jewels and silks, his camels white as milk, and horses with saddles stitched in gold, his menservants and his maidservants, and everything that was his.

Native talent for rigmarole asserted itself rather strongly up there. The night following the day spent at Carthage, I dreamed of the gazelle-eyed houri in the shadow of the tent, lovely enough to be the daughter born of the bridal of the earth and sky. I was deeply mortified and taken aback to learn next day that the pictorial group, her fiery kinsmen, camped in the shade of the palm grove, were a gang of gypsies. One sneaking scamp from among them tracked us half-way to Tunis, in hope of finding a chance to rob a straggler.

Fortunately, I did not mention my fancies -- so vivid, yet so weak -- to any one but you, my reader, and I know the secret is safe with you and will never go any further.

VII. DOING A LITTLE SHOPPING

"A MOOR from the bazaars with Mecca scarfs," said the polyglot courier at the Hotel d'Orient. I descended to the wide cool entrance-hall, a shady place, with stone floor and columns, and tiled wall, on which run verses of the Koran, inscribed in gilt letters on an azure background. In a land which knows little rain and never feels frost, its broad palace-like emptiness is inviting, albeit with a sense of homelessness to the Western traveller. At the furthest end, in the heavy shadow of magnolias without and lemon-trees within, stood a tall, straight, slender figure, his white turban in clear relief against the bright blue, -- the Moor with the Mecca scarfs. It is to be deplored that the influence of France in the East has exchanged graceful Oriental garments, flowing robes, and ample draperies for the rigid armor-like suits of the Parisian. This man I saw was true to the fierce traditions of his race, and was armed, as well as clad in the rich vestments of the gorgeous East; a barbaric magnificence, suited to the un-conquered people who never crouched before sovereigns, who had yoked kings to their chariots as beasts of burden, of whom the mighty Cambyses had to beg leave to pass through their dominions, and on whom even Sesostris and Cyrus could not impose conditions.

Imagination rallied from the stunning blow it had over night (from the gypsies, you remember, dear reader), and my very ideal of one half-civilized Asian prince stood before me, the hero of the most pathetic of human compositions. The noble Othello! For the first time I understood the gentle lady wedded to the Moor; how she could fall in love with what she had feared to look upon. By the bluest of seas, in some cool marble hall, with arabesque roof like this, Desdemona leaned against her father's breast to listen to the stories of regions of fable, mysteries, sorceries, and dim enchantments. Her household cares despatched in haste, she hung breathless on his words, her soul in her ears, tremblingly at first and in silence, rapt and gazing. "Her father loved me, oft invited me." This hero from the glowing zone came into her smooth, quiet, domestic life, like some brilliant tropic romance, and as the tragic tales went on, of feats of broil and battle, of moving accidents by flood and field, all the currents of her being set toward the regal stranger, who says, "I fetch my life and being from men of royal siege." He was robed in a sort of exotic grandeur by his princely bearing and military renown. That such as he, high-born, brave, and proud, should be sold to slavery, pained the innocent young heart and moved the hero to beguile her of her tears,

"WHEN I DID SPEAK OF SOME DISTRESSFUL STROKE
THAT MY YOUTH SUFFERED."

The passion for the marvellous and visionary is strong in women closely kept and guarded, and the shy, sensitive maiden was drawn as by subtle magnetism. He was not the tyrant of an Eastern seraglio; even Iago admits he was of a constant, loving, noble nature, till, being wrought, he disclosed the fierce fire of passion which flames in the blood of these children of the sun. Hers was the love which casteth out fear. She asked no questions, required no pledges.

"SHE LOVED ME FOR THE DANGERS I HAD PASSED,
AND I LOVED HER THAT SHE DID PITY THEM."

Swifter than light these thoughts flashed through my mind as I went down the stone stairs. Below the white turban I saw an olive face, with thin, sharp features; above, the eyes, those wonderful Asiatic eyes; the jet-black brows almost met; a beard of inky blackness, carefully smoothed, hid his throat. A short jacket, stiff with gold thread, was worn open in front, showing a vest embroidered with silks and stiff with gold; white linen trousers buttoned at the ankle; a variegated sash of vivid dyes, wrapped several times round his waist, held in place silver-mounted pistols and the crooked yataghan, in his hand a dreadful weapon.

A sort of handkerchief thrown over the turban had been removed and lay on the stranger's left arm, a many-colored mass, mainly crimson, with loose, long fringes in rich confusion, gay as the scarf of Iris. The Moor was strikingly handsome, picturesque, and dignified. He saluted by placing his hand on his breast, then touching it to his chin and forehead; a pretty movement, which has displaced the many prostrations and slow obeisances which were anciently the fashion among Orientals and still obtain in holy Damascus, the earthly Paradise of the Prophet. These men usually pick up a little French, but the noble Othello had only two words, "Madama Americana," -- the interpreter must do the rest. His pack of goods lay on the floor, like that of the New England pedler of a past generation; but, instead of hideous black oil-cloth or dirty old bed-ticking, the silken stuffs were enveloped in a square of buff cotton, a vine of green leaves wrought on its fringed edge. This was no pert, brisk Yankee trader with whom I was about to deal. I knew he would be slow as eternity; but I had ample leisure, and was not going to be overreached by him or any like him. Not I. Not if I know myself.

"Would Madama Americana be seated?" with a stately bow. She would. He then unrolled the bale and produced a gay little rug, which he spread for my slippered feet. He next brought a cigarette from his pocket, and not so much as saying, "By your leave," puffed away. "Madama does not smoke?" he said inquiringly. I replied my early education in that direction had been neglected. He nodded, much as to say, "Madama misses it mightily and is to be pitied." He then slowly drew out from the bottom of his pack a second rug, and seated himself on it quick as a wink, bringing his feet under him in a compact pose, impossible to one not to the manner born. The lithe, agile Arabian was used to the gesture, and the action had its own grace. I was forewarned. I knew these men have small capital and no credit; their whole stock of merchandise may be in the single bundle of modest size, bought out of a Greek brigantine for what he could pay and ready to be sold for what he could get. I knew the dealer would ask a towering price, hopelessly high, would lower inch by inch, and end by taking something in reason; besides, I believed the interpreter would give me a hint and not see me swindled, though he was an attaché of the Hotel d'Orient.

The noble Othello smoked in silence, sitting perfectly still. My patience and the cigarette were giving out together; as I was about to rise and leave, he tossed the cigar-stump into a small brass basin for the purpose standing near, and returned the amber holder to his pocket. He then drew his pack toward him, with the air of a man with abundant leisure and not to be hindered in the enjoyment of it, unfolded a short, wide scarf, and, with careless nonchalance, threw it on the striped mass covering his left arm. From that lustrous background it looked snowy white.

"It is from the sacred city of the Prophet, (may his name be extended far as the sand reaches!) and is made of the finest twilled silk."

I examined the fabric with care. It was very pretty, with striped gilt border and a thin gold fringe at the ends. When words are filtered through an interpreter, any needless speech seems folly. "What price?" I asked.

He named a sum equal to about forty-five dollars. I shook my head; but he regarded the shake coolly, as though I had shaken at the remotest stars. Evidently he was quite indifferent whether I bought or not. He went on serene as summer, smooth as society polish could make a man, this one whom we call barbarian.

"Will Madama lay the happy scarf round her head and throat, that she may feel its fine softness, like the furs of the north? It was made for the Princess Fatima Hammoun, niece of the Khedive of Egypt."

"Then how did you get possession of so costly a prize?"

"Ladies in the harems are sometimes short of money." said the unconcerned trader, softly, waving the gauzy silk in air. "The Madama Americana may strike off my head if I speak not the truth. Perhaps this will suit her better." He shook out a long, light woollen shawl, of dull apple-green. "Such was the turban of Mohammed (exalted be his name!) when in the heat of battle he raised it on a lance and made the green banner forever sacred." With stately reverence he inclined toward the royal colors and laid it by the white scarf.

"What price?" I asked.

"Seventy-five dollars."

I shook my head with energy. "Possibly Madama Americana would like some towels? Here are the towels of Damascus, embroidered with gold. They come from Araby the Blest, and are fresh from the last caravan."

"Will they wash?"

"Forever. The silk is the best of Syria, and the broidery was laid on in delightful gardens by the flowery banks of the Pharpar. It will be shining ten thousand years hence, as now, and is such as Ayesha, the beautiful wife, worked for the Apostle of God. Will Madama make me proud to look at them? The Bey of Tunis has this day ordered fifteen dozen, as a present to the Sultan Abdul Hamid the Beloved. May he sleep safe in the Yildiz Palace, by the Bosphorus."

Really, this pedler of the East had the imagination of a poet, the grace of a courtier, and the will of a conqueror. Again I thought of the fatal handkerchief in the hand of the Moor of Venice, in whose web there was magic, --

"THAT HANDKERCHIEF
DID AN EGYPTIAN TO MY MOTHER GIVE.
SHE WAS A CHARMER.
THE WORMS WERE HALLOWED THAT DID BREED THE SILK,
AND IT WAS DYED IN MUMMY, WHICH THE SKILFUL
CONSERVED OF MAIDENS' HEARTS."

These people manage to give a fictitious value to each piece of merchandise they offer. Like the handkerchief spotted with strawberries, it has associations more precious than the goods. It is *antica* -- that is, antique -- from some old mosque, or a *facsimile* of one worn by goddess, queen, or sultana, or other august personage, whose very name stirs the fancy. The noble Othello leaned his back against the wall, resting from what toils I could not know. "Are you from the khan of Sadullah Bey?" I asked. "Sadullah buys of me," said the unmoved merchant, in haughty scorn, eying his small bundle with pride enough for a whole Magasin du Louvre. I think the Arabian was irritated at the question, for the luminous eyes glowed like burning coals. A dead pause of five long minutes, and he began again. "Madama sees here the choice things fit for those who live in the shadow of lofty palaces; but remember," he said gravely, as he slowly refolded the green banner, "four things come not back, -- the spoken word, the sped arrow, the past life, the neglected opportunity. Thus sayeth the proverb." The golden embroidery was in mystic hieroglyph along the edges of the holy flag. "From the Koran," said the Moslem, devoutly sliding a lean brown finger along the lines: "pure gold -- it will never dim, and water does not tarnish it, nor time, though it last ten thousand years."

"It is too dear. I may look at the towels again." He lifted one and threw it on the near divan. "This is from Bagdad, -- from Bagdad, the land of Aladdin, of Sindbad and Zobeide, Scheherezade, the rose and the nightingale, of ivory and amber, spicery and richest merchandise. The tempter saw my wavering. Those keen eyes lost nothing and marked every shade of change, without seeming to see anything.

"Beware of the neglected opportunity," said the born-and-bred fatalist, beguilingly. "God, the merciful, ordains all things, and only once in a lifetime come the great chances, according as Kismet has prepared them. *Allah kerim!*"

By this time the servants of the hotel, several idlers and travellers, had come round to watch the trade, and formed a ring, of which the Moor, the interpreter, and your correspondent were the centre. Not a word was uttered nor a sign made. They looked on intently, apparently anxious, as though the fate of thousands was in the venture. I sent an appealing glance at the interpreter, who pretended not to see. I could not spend the whole day in bargaining. The delay was tedious; the situation embarrassing to a woman not used to Eastern ways. "What for the towel?"

"The towel from Bagdad? Twelve dollars."

"Too much."

"Then will Madama make an offer? Americanas are princesses. Their money comes easy and goes fast. Offer?"

"Six dollars," I said hastily, for I wanted to get rid of the man, and he had stayed so long I felt obliged to buy something and "Jewing" is not my forte. It was the Moor's turn to shake his head now, which he did in melancholy and decorous fashion, not tending to unsettle the turban folded with graceful coils above the olive forehead, which it nearly concealed. The neglected opportunity -- was I missing it? A towel from Bagdad is hot in market every day, and it would be a nice souvenir. The chance was passing, the supreme moment, the neglected opportunity.

"Six dollars!" I said recklessly.

"I lose money," said the melancholy man, imploring by mournful accent and wistful gesture.

"I cannot help it," I retorted, warming with the day. "You need not sell if you don't want to."

"A man hard pressed must take what he can get. It is Kismet. The towel is yours. It will please Madama's friends across the sea, beyond the Straits. May it be like the enchanted carpet of Boudressein, which brought a fresh good fortune to its owner every morning."

"Have I seen your stock of goods?"

"You have," he replied, much as to say, "The world is at your feet; what more can mortal ask?" The interpreter counted the money, the crowd broke away, smiling and jabbering in half a dozen languages, and one Neapolitan remarked in French: "A runner from Sadullah Bey's. A man not pleasant to meet, if one has anything to lose." The noble Othello alone preserved his calm dignity, and in silence made his courteous, profound salaam. When his few goods were gathered, he leaned his back against the wall, after the manner of people who love repose, looking little like one ready to mount horse and draw sabre for Islam, willing every hour to die for his faith. Somehow the noble Othello's bearing made me feel like a robber, and, with a sense of guilt, I turned to the stairs with the spoil. My heart sank. My feminine reader will weep with me when I tell her the first unfolding of the Persian towel revealed several stout coffee-stains, which added dirt to the yellow tint which dulled its beauty and freshness. What a forlorn purchase I had made! Had I been cheated by a strolling pedler, after all the warning fingers lifted at me on both sides the sea? I? *I?*

Thalia was lying in wait for me on a divan in the balconied window. I have a shrewd suspicion she had been listening over the banister, but she looked innocent as a baby. There was no chance of hiding the bargain which had been conducted with so much dignity and ceremony. I walked toward her, trying to assume a careless manner, and plunged boldly into the subject by flaunting the embroidery before her eyes, thereby revealing two holes hidden with consummate art and a wretched spot where the fringe stopped short at one end; and oh! what were those mysterious dots all over the scant and meagre fabric? Thalia smiled such an ironic, blighting sarcasm of a smile as I never saw in her face before. It covered me with confusion, and made my splendid Bagdad towel dwindle and shrink to the proportions of a doyley. "Ah! I see your rage for antiquities again. This has arrived at the antique, without becoming a gem, hasn't it?" She held it up to the light, which it slightly obstructed, showing a "body" like the sleazy stuff our grandmothers used to make milk-strainers of.

"Don't you think it's rather -- rather thin?" she continued, the dimples deepening in her cheeks. "And, dear me, what did you pay a fly-speck?" She broke into the gayest laugh in the world.

I reddened with vexation, but was dumb. She took the Bagdad towel in her two little hands, gave a slight jerk, and the rotten old thing split from one end to the other.

"Really, now, that is too bad! I bought this as a souvenir for you, a sample of Oriental magnificence, and you have gone and ruined it!"

"Thank you, kindly," said the spoilt beauty, burying her laughter in the pillows; "but I always prefer my dish-rags without tinsel."

VIII. THE LIGHT OF THE HAREM – PART I

IT was in the land of crumbling cities, strange religions, deserted fanes; of quiet men, in twisted turbans and long beards; of placid women, with faces shrouded like the faces of the dead, as pale and as calm. Tranquil prisoners, with respite to drive and walk about the streets, and for a brief space of time escape bolt and bars, in charge of armed attendants. A land silent as though Time himself had dropped to sleep and broken his emptied hour-glass.

By the bluest and clearest of seas there is a deep bay, where the navies of the world might ride at anchor. The sweeping curves of its shores are drawn as by an artist's hand, and from its margin rise terraced heights, like the hanging gardens of Babylon. Toward the west are hills, with capes of olive green, from which the breeze blows deliriously cool in the hottest days. Away to the south tall, slim minarets point toward the glittering god of the ancient Persian, and dwarf the rounded domes below by the ethereal grace of their tapering spires. Close to the water's edge stands a palace worthy the golden prime of Haroun al Raschid, nobly built of white and pink marble, the latter brought from Egypt. In the distance, under a sky that would be dazzling were it not so soft, it shines like a temple of alabaster and silver.

Its crowning glory is a central dome, rising in peerless beauty, like a globe of ice or of crystal, and seeming to hang in air. Mirrored in the glassy water, the plume-like pillars and slender turrets are a picture to make one in love with its builder. He had the soul of an artist who measured the span of its rhythmic arches and told the heights of its colonnades, harmonious to the eye as choice music to the ear. He must have toiled years to embody in this result his study of the beautiful. The architect was a Spaniard, and he had the same creative faculty (this man who worked in formless stone) that the poet has who brings his idea out of hidden depths, polishes his work with elaborate care, nor leaves it till every line is wrought to perfect finish. Under a despotic government architecture that is magnificent flourishes, though all other arts languish. Among a semi-civilized people kings prefer this expression of power, because it is readily understood, demanding no instruction, no book or guide. He who runs may read, be it the stupendous monument of Cheops or the airy pinnacles of Solyman the Magnificent. The wish is to give form which shall compel the entire people to admiring astonishment of works they cannot hope to imitate.

Let us call this the Palace of Delight, for there dwells in the luxury and aroma of the furthest East Nourmahal, the Light of the Harem, and we were invited to see her, -- the bulbul. the rose, the Pearl of the Orient, the bride of Prince Feramorz. Dear reader, do you know how come the brides in this strange country? Do you think it a wooing of an innocent, laughing girl, who, as in lands of social freedom, lays her light hand, with her heart in it, in yours? A prize won in an emulous game, where beauty is weighed against all beside which the world has to offer, and he who has the right divine may carry her off from Love's shining circle to be the centre of another of his own creation. There was no flavor of American matches in this betrothal, no hint of golden afternoons in shady lanes, nights of moonlit silence, and dreams better than sleep, of wedding bells in festal rooms, and orange flowers that leave a sweetness outlasting the waste of years. Nor was it like European marriages, -- say the French or Italian, -- where a demure young girl is taken from the convent, and by her parents given to the most eligible *parti*, of whom she is not allowed an opinion, whom she sees not one hour alone till after the ceremony, in which her *dot* is the first, second, and third consideration.

Nor yet is it brought about like the weddings in kings' palaces, by negotiations for babies in the cradle, long, tedious betrothal, interviews at proper times, in proper places, and presences appointed, where exact proprieties are observed by the happy or unhappy pair. Nor was the contract made as of old, in plains not very far distant from this, when Abraham sent out his most trusted servant as a business agent -- a travelling man, if you please -- seeking a bride for his son Isaac. By no such devious windings did our princess come to the altar. The lovely Nourmahal was bought at private sale for ten thousand pieces of gold, and thus the marriage was accomplished. It is not our business to inquire whether the bargain was made in the shadow of the black tents of the Bedouin, or on frosty heights of Caucasus, or in some verdant vale in Araby the Blest. It was to a better condition, came she from dissolute races, like the Georgian or barbarian hordes, like the Tartar and Circassian, where the bride's portion is a sheepskin, a sack of barley, a hand-mill, and an earthen pan. It was a moment of melancholy disenchantment when I first learned how she had reached the rank and power of princess, by what means been lifted from desert sand and gypsy poverty to eider down and silken luxury, and made a true believer, walking in the paths of the faithful. To be young, beautiful, and beloved is Heaven; she was this, and, it was said, sweet as summer cherries withal.

Our amiable inquiries about what is not our concern availed little. Her history was colorless till the fated hour came when its blank page should be illuminated and glow with tropic splendor. She was a chosen beauty; princes seldom sigh in vain; and, so long as men have eyes to see, fair women will wear purple and sit on thrones.

Our names were sent in ten days before the reception, a day which stands apart in memory in the year 1881, in the Time of the Scattering of Roses, or, as we would say, in the month of August.

The heaviest iron-clads might lie close to the quay where we landed. So pure is the water and so intensely clear that, at the depth of four fathoms, fish swim and bright stones lie as though close beneath the calm surface. Marble steps lead to the water; and when our little boat neared them two sentinels, moveless as statues, appeared, clad in the picturesque costume of the Tunisian *kavasse*; all gold embroidery and dazzling color, even to the holsters of pistols and the sides of the long-topped boots. A wall, perhaps thirty feet high, made of rough stone, was broken by a gate of iron, light as network, evidently of French construction. Its double valves flew open at our approach, and as quickly closed when we entered the garden. Two jet-black attendants were in waiting, from that degraded class of men to whom princes safely trust their treasures. The word "harem" means "the reserved," and these were part of the reserve guard, -- hideous Ethiops of the extremest type, with flattened nose and lips, -- swollen rolls of dingy flesh.

Their misshapen skulls were hidden by that singular formation called a fez. When the Creator gave these creatures life, he denied them all else. Condemned by nature to a perpetual mourning suit, they had revenge in gorgeous costume, which must have been consoling. To perfect their ugliness, both were badly pitted with small-pox. After the long-continued obeisances of the East, they stood with folded arms and downcast eyes, fixed as the stone lions beside the gate.

The garden was small, the narrow walks paved with black and white pebbles, laid in graceful Arabesque patterns, rimmed with a fanciful border of tiles. We had scented, out in the bay, the heavy fragrance of roses we call damask: masses of bloom, crowded in beds or lining alleys reddened by their blossoms. The terraces were high and narrow, their sheer sides banks of ivy, honeysuckle, and myrtle; a tangle of running vines giving the feeling of wildness and seclusion in its untamed luxuriance. There the acacia "waved her yellow hair," most exquisite of trees, delicate as some high-born lady, a frail beauty in her trembling lace-work of fine leaves. Beneath its branches was a swing of manilla cord, with a cushion tasselled and fringed with gold. Bees hummed, butterflies darted through the air like flying leaves, and humming-birds hovered over purple bells of a creeper to me unknown.

Up higher were dense shades of laurel and lemon, pomegranate, with scarlet buds, close thickets of bay and of citron, walks set with daisies and violets, bordered by heliotrope and lavender. Highest on the hill, accented with clear outline against the speckless sapphire, stood the round-topped cedars of the Orient, reminders of Lebanon, and the palm, swaying its green plumes. Most honored of trees, for, says the devout Moslem, "Thou must honor thy paternal aunt, the date palm, for she was created of the earth of which Adam was made." In the centre of the garden a fountain threw a glancing column skyward and fell in an alabaster basin, where gold fish swam among white lilies and the azure lotus of Persia. A tiny stream, brought from the snowy sides of some distant mountain, ran in wayward grace over vari-colored pebbles, laid with studied carelessness and nicest attention to effect, a copy of nature. On its rim a long-legged stork stood, intent on his prey. A miniature pavilion, a gracious retreat from the sun was roofed with vines, from which hung pendent the scarlet passion flower. Oh! it was beautiful! beautiful! All flowers consecrated by poetry, religion, and love grew there. Even the rough wall was covered like the verdurous wall of the first garden, which lay eastward in Eden. Could it be possible the trail of the serpent is over it all? Rather let me believe it the Earthly Paradise of the Prophet or the Paradise Regained of the Christian.

We could not loiter, for Nourmahal was waiting. From the entrance hall to which men are admitted, called "the place of greeting," slave girls emerged to meet us and drew up in lines, through which we passed. We crossed an outer court, open to the sky, with cool marble pavement, under an arched way, to a hall covered with India matting. Beyond was a spacious rotunda, a fountain dancing in the centre under the dome, which rested on pillars of lapis lazuli. I counted eight fragile supporting columns of bright blue veined with white. Overhead were traceries in blue and gold, pendent stalactites, the "honeycomb ceilings" of the Moorish kings; the tints of the Alhambra were in the inlaying of many colors, and gilt texts of the Koran on the walls. The builder had that most romantic of castles in heart and eye when he planned the Palace of Delight. We slowly crossed the circular space (everything moves slowly here), stopping only to admire a sultana bird, with purple breast, in an ivory cage, and a few white doves, that with many a flirt and flutter bathed in the bright water or on the rim of the pool, cooed and twined their beaks together, with outstretched wings, undisturbed by our approach. Beyond was the reception room, called Dares-Saadet (Abode of Felicity), where the Pearl of the Orient was to be seen. It was screened by a *portiére* made of Lahore shawls, figured with palm leaves, elephants, and pagodas, -- a quaint and costly drapery, drawn back for us to pass under. As we entered, a crowd of slave girls formed lines, between which we passed; young natives from the mountains of the Atlas, with vicious eyes and sidelong glances. One was a light mulatto, with crisp hair and downcast look, reminding me of the old days of slavery. They were dressed in cheap, gay, checked silks, made like our morning wrappers; belts of tinsel, large silver earrings, with grotesque heads of animals in front. White muslin turbans covered their heads, their hands were thin and wiry, and they bore the meek, passive manner of all women of the East. Two sides of the room were of glass, the one overlooking the bay latticed with iron, painted white, which banished the prison look it would otherwise have. Velvety rugs of Bochara and Korassan were laid here and there over the floor of blue and white mosaic. A broad, low divan of pale blue silk ran round the apartment. *Voilá tout.* No pictures on the marble walls, no books, no *bric-á-brac*, no trumpery "collections," ceramics, aesthetic trash, grave or gay, nor muffling hangings. These are not Oriental luxuries; but, instead, a cool, shady emptiness, plenty of space for the breeze to flutter the gauzy curtains and carry the echo of the plash and drip of the fountains.

At the furthest end, reclining on pillows of silk and lace, rested the lady we sought. One little foot, in red velvet slipper, was first seen below wide trousers of yellow silk; a loose robe of white silk, embroidered with gold thread, was partly covered by a sleeveless jacket of crimson, dotted with seed pearl; a broad variegated sash wound the slender waist. Half concealing the arms was a light scarf, airy as the woven wind of the ancients. A head-band, with diamond pendants, fringed her forehead; a *rivière* of diamonds circled the bare throat; and here and there solitary drops flashed in the braids of her night-black hair. Among the billowy cushions and vaporous veilings rose the young face -- oh, what a revelation of beauty! -- uplifted in a curious, questioning way, to see what manner of women these are, who come from the ends of the earth, with unveiled faces, and go about the world alone, and have to think for themselves, -- poor things! The expression was that of a lovely child, waking from summer slumber in the happiest humor, ready for play. A sensitive, exquisite face, fair as the first of women while the angel was yet unfallen. A perfect oval, the lips a scarlet thread, and oh, those wonderful Asiatic eyes! -- lustrous, coal-black, long, rather than round, beaming under the joined eyebrows of which the poet Hafiz sings.

The edges of the eyelids were blackened with kohl, which Orientals use to intensify the brilliance of the brightest eyes under the sun. The most common kind is smoke-black, made by burning frankincense or shells of almonds. Sometimes an ore of lead is used in fine powder. Our American girls make a miserable bungle of it, smearing the whole eyelids, giving a ghastly and unnatural effect, very different from the thin line of antimony, applied by a probe of ivory, dipped in the powder and skilfully drawn on the tip edges of the lids.

IX. THE LIGHT OF THE HAREM - PART II

NOURMAHAL did not rise, but held out one jewelled hand, dimpled as a baby's, with nails and finger-ends dyed pink with henna, -- five clustering rosebuds. The magic of beauty made us her subjects. We kissed the little fingers loyally, and yielded ourselves willing captives, ready to be dragged at her chariot-wheels. My life-long notions of the subjection of woman (see Stuart Mill) and the wretchedness of prisoners pining in palatial splendors vanished at the first glance; went down at a touch, like the wounded knight in the lists of Templestowe. She smiled, and hoped we were well; then followed suitable inquiries as to health and journeys, and expressions of the charm of finding it all out. Our interpreter was an Armenian lady, with the gift of tongues. When conversation is filtered through three languages, it becomes very thin; even such bold and spirited remarks as, "This is a happy day for me; I shall never forget it," was robbed of half its spice and flavor by the time it reached the ear for which it was intended. I ventured the high assertion that we had sailed six thousand miles on purpose to lay our homage at her blessed feet; which rhetorical flourish was received with a childish nod at about what it was worth. Somehow, she did not seem so enchanted with her new worshippers as they were with her. It appeared the Beauty had never seen the sea except from shore.

"What is it like when you are in the middle of the dark water?"

"Had she seen the Great Desert?"

"Yes, many times, and had trembled when awful columns of dust swept across it, moved by the wings of evil genii."

"It was like that; wide, still, a desert of water more lonely than any land."

"Do many people drown there?" she asked of the mysterious horror.

"Very few. You would have no fear."

"Because I shall never go on it," she said triumphantly, and laughed, showing teeth like pomegranate seeds, and shook the diamond drops on her forehead, so delighted was she with the simple wit.

Suddenly changing her tone, she asked, "Why do you wear black dresses?"

I have never seen an Eastern woman, of high or low degree, in a black garment of any make. Even their shoes are gayly embroidered. Dismal and coarse three elderly women, in the conventional black silks and poke bonnets, must appear to one clad in elegant draperies of various and brilliant dyes, whose eyes ever rested on tints to which the rainbow is dim.

"It is the custom of our country for women to go out in black," we answered.

"How sad!" said Beauty; and it did seem sad in that light and lovely room, all sunshine and vivid color. We were in love with her, and again declared our love. She accepted the admiration as one well used to such extravagance, and clapped her hands after the fashion of ladies of the "Arabian Nights." At the signal, the slaves disappeared, except one old woman and the Negroes, silent as ghosts, beside the Lahore drapery. In a few minutes five slaves returned, each carrying a small round table of cedar, inlaid with scraps of mother of pearl. Five others followed, with lighted cigarettes, lying each in a silver saucer; and coffee in tiny cups, about the size of a giant's thimble, resting in a silver filigree holder, set round with diamonds.

"My new friends have come so far," said Nourmahal, "they must be tired. Take a cigarette and refresh yourselves."

I rather awkwardly adjusted the holder of amber and ventured one faint whiff. Imagine my astonishment at seeing my friend, whose name with difficulty I suppress, puff away like a dissipated old smoker. The Armenian was native and to the manner born. Nourmahal smoked, of course, and a lulling calm succeeded the excitement of the brilliant conversation reported above. While feeling round in my brain for a subject of common interest adapted to our hostess's capacity and mine, I tried a sip of the coffee. It was strong enough to bear up an egg, thick with grounds, and bitter as death. I pretended to deep enjoyment of the dose, and sipped it, drop by drop, to the bitter end.

Nourmahal clapped her hands again, and the ten virgins took away the saucers. I think none of them were foolish, for they fell into line without effort, each one treading in the footsteps of her predecessor, at an interval to avoid her train.

Presently they returned, with gold-fringed napkins and silver cups of sherbet, flavored with quince, and a conserve of rose-leaves. Wishing to appear easy as possible and thoroughly Oriental, I trifled with the delicious nectar, cooled with snow, and was not half through when the attendant picked up my table of cedar and pearl and disappeared with it. How

I regret not having swallowed the Olympian food at railroad speed, for it was the first ice I had seen for many months. It is not court etiquette to ask receipts, and, after a sigh of regret for what I shall never taste again, I returned to the fascination of a triple-tongued conversation.

"In this charming palace you must be very happy. How do you pass the time?"

The dimples deepened in the cheeks of Beauty. "Pass the time, pass the time?" she dreamily repeated, playing with the knotted fringes of her scarf. "I do not pass it, it passes itself!" and again she laughed, and the laughter was sweet as the tenderest voice can make it.

"Are you fond of music?"

Three ladies in black: "Oh! very!" "Oh! very!" "Oh! very!"

"Then you shall be amused." She clapped the rose-leaf palms, and in marched eight women musicians (we saw no men that day but the harem guard), bearing stringed instruments. Curious-looking things, like overgrown violins and half-finished guitars, and a round shell, with strings across, beaten with two sticks.

Didst ever hear Arabic music, beloved?

No? Then never hast thou known sorrow.

Since Jubal first struck the gamut, there can have been no improvement in these compositions. How long the exercises lasted I am unable to record; but I do know we grew old fast under the beat, beat, hammer, hammer, in the terse, unmeaning notes of the banjo. In the brief interval, at the end of a peculiarly agonizing strain, sung by the mulatto, I seized the moment to ask what were the words of the song, and was told it is a serenade, very ancient, dating back to the Times of Ignorance, before the coming of Mohammed, whose tomb is covered with the splendor of unceasing light. I afterward obtained a copy of the madrigal and give it in rough translation. It is doubtful if the almond-eyed Juliet came down from her lattice after the anguish of that performance on the *vina*.

GAZZEL; OR, LOVE SONG.

ON A STEED SHOD WITH FIRE I COME,
AND WEARY IS MY HEART WITH WAITING.
AWAKENED IT FEELS A VAGUE UNREST.

    CHORUS:
O THOU WHOSE SHAPE IS THAT OF THE CYPRESS,
AND WHOSE MOUTH IS THE OPENING ROSEBUD,
I AM HERE, FAITHFUL AS THY SHADOW.

THY EYEBROWS ARE THE FORM OF AN ARCH,
THE SHAFTS OF THY LASHES ARE UNSPARING,
AND THE SCARS WHICH THEY LEAVE ARE BLEEDING.
    O THOU WHOSE SHAPE, ETC.

QUEEN ROSE, THY SLAVE RASCHID IS BEGGARED.
HIS WHOLE HEART IS ONLY ONE WOUND;
SMILE BUT ONCE AND HIS HEAD WILL TOUCH THE STARS.
    O THOU WHOSE SHAPE, ETC.

After the serenade followed a battle song, which made our blood tingle with its fierce din. It was of a victorious chief, who had been far as Istamboul, the pearl of two seas, the possession of which is the longing desire of every monarch. The singer imitated the clanking keys of conquered cities, and sang of jewelled turbans worn by padishas, of gold and perfumes, ivory and balsam, of kiosks smelling of musk, ceiled with cedar, and painted with vermilion.

Then the theme changed to a melancholy minor key. The bright warrior, named Yilderinn, or Lightning, so strong and swift was he, is wounded and going to die; he who, if the sky were to fall, could uphold it on the point of his lance. He salutes the black angel in the patient resignation to sorrow, which the

Prophet of God says is the key to all happiness. "Weep not for him; he is tasting the honey of martyrdom, the reward of those who fall fighting for Islam. Weep not for him who has the passport to Paradise. In place of two hands lost in defending the standard of the faith, two wings are given to bear him across the dread bridge El Sirat, to the blissful regions where sixty black-eyed houris and endless Elysian pleasures await every true believer. He is passing to their gardens, the Dwelling of the Blest." A droning recitative, with tuneless, timeless accompaniment on the two-stringed guitar.

Then came a burst of triumphant chords which made our flesh creep. The bright warrior has angelic visions and hears angelic voices: "I see, I see a dark-eyed girl! She has dropped the flowered veil from her starlike eyes, and waves a handkerchief, a handkerchief of green, and smiles and shouts: 'Come kiss me, kiss me, for I love thee.' Keep watch by me to-night, O Death; come and keep watch by me." The concluding line trailed off in a dying way, and died in a succession of heart-breaking moans.

My smoking friend looked deadly pale, as though about to faint, and whispered, "An air from 'Pinafore' would be a relief." It struck me that any air would be a relief to her in that desperate extremity. How I envied Nourmahal, who adjusted her lace and silken pillows, and, nestled in them, had dropped into a gentle nap. When the last blow hit my tired tympanum, up she rose from rainbow scarfs and frothy veilings, like Aphrodite from the mist and foam of the sea, and, without apology, said to the Armenian lady, "The audience is ended."

We were not sorry. Our limited supply of words forbade the giving of "views," so dear to the mind of the universal suffragist; but we had enough to repeat offers of service and protest vows of remembrance, which the princess received in a listless way, much as to say, "This thing grows tiresome." I think she was a little mortified at the siesta, which led to such a protracted session of the rub-a-dub music. To hear is to obey was the law of all around her, and, had she slept on till morning, there was no one to stop the work of the band of torturers.

As we passed out of the salon, each of us received a box of crimson andem wood, wrapped in tissue paper. "To be opened when you reach home," said the interpreter.

The doves had gone to their nests, for the shades of evening were in the rotunda; the sultana bird, with head under its wing, was a purple ball; the moon was high over the enchanted garden, which the King of the Genii had made for Prince Feramorz. A tame gazelle, wearing a collar of silver bells, followed us to the gate, and in a fond, endearing way laid its pretty head on my arm and looked in my face. The most appealing glance of a weary prisoner, longing for the freedom of Judah's hills, the mild thyme of Hermon, and the mountains of spices. Those eyes had a human expression, which has never left my memory. I have seen it in the wistful gaze of young mothers, in the yearning eyes of those who have so long mourned that the grief has become a softened sorrow. Well do they name the love song "Gazelle."

Before the gate we suddenly paused, at the same instant, moved by the same impulse, and turned to look for one moment more on the Palace and Garden of Delight. We felt we should not see its like again, for there are few such gardens in the world. The Paradise palms were whispering their secrets, and the pines wailed in answer to the sea breeze as harp-strings answer to the harper's hand. The moonlight tipped each leaf with silver; the flowers were pale, but not faded; heaven and earth were still, breathless, as we grow when feeling most. A bird, a little brown thing, like a wren, flew out of a thicket of laurels and hid among the starry blossoms of the magnolia. Then hark! that wondrous note. I should have recognized it even if Thalia had not lifted a hushing finger and said, under her breath, "Believe me, love, it is the nightingale."

It *was* the nightingale, and the voice (so sweet, so sweet, I hear it yet, and shall hear it at intervals forever) was more stilling than very silence. That wild melody was not the legendary plaint of the lovelorn mate, leaning her breast against a thorn, but rather an ecstatic strain from a soul so full it must tell its rapture or die. Its charm was past all telling, beyond the reach of words. Still, as I write, hundreds of miles away, after months of rapid travel, my heart thrills with the echo of its ineffable sweetness. The doe (the winsome thing, with the haunting eyes) leaned heavily against my arm while we stood and listened. Night was fallen, for in these latitudes it makes brief mingling with day. It is only to meet and kiss in a crimson blush and part again. "Good-by forever," we said, as the lock snapped in the iron valves. The voice of the bulbul followed us through the perfumed dusk, like an invisible angel allowed to pass the guarded gates of Eden and cheer the homely pilgrims on their way.

Freshly the breeze blew, and the briny smell of the sea was tonic, after the languors of the palace. The rich and balmy eve invited to silence. Under a trance we floated between blue and blue (whether in the body or out of the body I cannot tell) in the supreme delight of a day unreal in its poetic lights; so like the stuff which dreams are made of, I sometimes wonder which was dream and which reality.

From the distant minaret sounded a long musical wail, that seemed to fall from vague regions surrounding us, or as a warning voice from some unseen world, close at hand, the muezzin's call to prayer. When it died away, a second voice took up the cry, another followed, and another, as trumpets answer and echo among far-off friendly camps. It was finer than the stirring appeal of bugles, clearer than the ringing bells of Christendom. These were the words wafted through the ethereal haze, across the halcyon sea, revealed in vision to the Prophet: "God is great! God is great! There is no God but God. Mohammed is the apostle of God. Come to prayers! Come to prayers! Prayer is better than sleep! *Alla hu!*"

A light pleasure-boat approached, with striped canopy, and bearing a colored lantern, like a great red eye, in front. Ten men bent to the oars, it flew across the water, and phosphorescent light fell off the dripping blades like sparkles of fire. It came nearer, and we knew, by the crescent and shining star in the flag, it was an official of high rank, -- the solitary passenger seated in the slender bow among restful cushions. The fez cap has no brim. As the bark shot past, we knew the boyish face, and caught one glance of the imperial eyes of Prince Feramorz.

When the call ended, he knelt, and, without shame or concealment, prostrated his forehead to the floor, his face toward Mecca, the Holy City of the Faithful. Here is the prayer, named Fatiyeh, which pious Moslems repeat five times a day: --

"Praise be to God, the Lord of all creatures, the most merciful, the King of the Day of Judgment! Thee do we worship, and of Thee do we beg assistance. Direct us in the right way, in the way of those to whom Thou hast been gracious, not of those against whom Thou hast been incensed nor of those who go astray; "--

the prayer which Adam uttered after his expulsion from Eden, that Abraham said after his son was saved from sacrifice, that Christ breathed in the Gethsemane agony, so they tell us, as it is written in the books of the Chronicles.

X. THE LIGHT OF THE HAREM – PART III

WHEN we reached the hotel we had a tolerable supper of foreign dishes, mixed with rice and flavorless, as that tasteless vegetable makes everything it touches. Then in wrappers, comfortable as could be without ice-water or rocking-chairs, we reviewed the day's pleasure and opened our presents. Thalia's was an automatic bird of iridescent glass, which could be made to sing by winding with a key. My smoking friend, who, it is safe to say, will never smoke again, had a box of delicious French bonbons, which melt in your mouth, almost in your glance. The Armenian's was a necklace of Egyptian coins and filigree silver; mine a pendant in green enamel. I touched the spring, the locket flew open, and lo! the serene, pictorial face of Nourmahal. I held the portrait close to the quaint brass lamp (an Aladdin pattern), and we looked at the faultless features in unmixed admiration. "She is, indeed, the Light of the Harem," murmured the smoker.

The Advanced Thinker, eldest of the party, one of the bravest of the brave American women, turned to her and said, "What a pity we could not plant a few ideas in that childish brain!"

"What sort of ideas would you like to plant?" asked the other, dryly, without releasing the matchless face from her gaze.

Advanced Thinker, in a tone of solemn authority: "That life is made for something more than being sweet and sleepy."

"You would have her sour and wide-awake, then, would you? and for your sowing reap a harvest of discontent? Do you think it would help the happiness of that house to-night, when Prince Feramorz comes home, to find her bothering over development and evolution? She does all her husband demands, which is to be beautiful and kind. I know what you want," she continued, warming, and with rapidly rising voice. "You want her to study those awful problems about the fox and the greyhound, and the cistern with two pipes, and to read Buckle and Darwin, and worry about rights and wrongs, and have views and give them, too, and make speeches, and, in short, to be wise -- and wretched."

"As to speeches," said the Advanced Thinker, also very dry, "many are called to the platform, but few are chosen." (She is a first-rate leader in women's-rights conventions.) "Nourmahal should, at least, know she is a responsible being, and that every human soul has some divinely appointed work, which only that one can accomplish. A perfect Talmud of tradition is walled about these Oriental women. They are fettered with bands of brass."

"Nourmahal is fettered with rosy garlands," retorted the smoker, hotly. "She is an innocent child, working out her destiny, which is to give and receive happiness, to twine and vine, sing and cling and swing, instead of straining up hills more or less imaginary and battling prejudices old and fixed as Mount Sinai.

As your own Joseph Cook would say, she is in harmonization with her environments. Let her alone." And the speaker closed the locket with an emphatic snap. It was as though a lovely light went out.

It was my turn now. "Dear friend," I said, "do you see three lines between my eyebrows? Strangers newly arrived in our country declare they are the distinguishing feature of the American woman."

"It must be confessed -- "she said, hesitating.

"Nonsense," I said, interrupting. "Are they or are they not there?"

"If you will have it, even the eyes of love must admit that three faint lines --"

"Faint! Speak the truth, child, as under oath."

"Well, to pacify you, three well-defined lines appear between your eyebrows."

"Precisely. They are, as you say, well defined, and their definition is free agency, universal suffrage, and aesthetic culture."

I opened the sweet picture again and held it up.

"Would you mark them in that untroubled face between the even brows of the youngest of the Graces?"

"Not I. A butterfly is as good in its way as an old hen. For my part, I find it refreshing to meet a woman content to be what she is, -- the dimple on the cheek of home. She is more like Eve in her bower than any one I have ever seen. She is not made of common clay, but of bright gems, as Mohammedans say the angels are made."

"Merely a grown-up baby," continued the Advanced Thinker, with cold, severe insistence. "I suppose she doesn't know how to read or to sew."

"It would be a shame," sharply struck in Thalia, "to put a pen in those rosebud fingers, to dull the lustre of her eyes over crabbed dictionaries and grammars. If she reads the gay texts of the Koran on the walls, it is enough to live by and die by. Why harp on cerebral action and the abysses of the unknowable? I am tired of all this talk about life's discipline. It is sure to find you out." She went on vehemently, raising her voice to the ledger-lines above, while she rolled up her crimps: "Instead of making the world a place of rational enjoyment, it is insisted you must have an object and go on three-score years working for that object; and what does the object bring, but vanity and vexation of spirit? The words 'sense of duty' have forever driven out sense of love, and it is harder for each new generation. We go deeper and deeper into the toil and trouble, because the terrible duties keep rolling up in size and weight. Protoplasm, pangenesis, and the rest of it -- after all, the world is no wiser. No man to-day writes as well as Job or Moses; no woman can sing like Miriam. The strain on women is so severe, as the ideal standard grows higher, that the march of the ages of which we hear so much has become a dead march, and the records are written on stones over untimely graves."

Advanced Thinker, mildly, but speaking with energy: "What qualities has little Baby-face to hold Prince Feramorz with when youth and beauty have vanished?"

"He will see her still beautiful, with the eyes of memory and habit," replied Thalia, with earnest feeling, her blue eyes moistening. "There are sympathies and experiences which outlast the fleeting spell of beauty; magnetisms beyond mere attractions of person. You know the old story, which is the best thing told of Mohammed. With all the world to choose from, he never swerved from his early allegiance to Kadijah, the wife of his youth, older than himself and never beautiful.

"'O Apostle of God,' said Ayesha, the bride of his house, but not of his heart, 'was not Kadijah stricken in years? Has not Allah given thee a better wife in her place?'

"'A fairer; but a better -- never!' said Mohammed. 'Never did God give man a better. When I was poor, she enriched me; when I was called a liar, she believed in me; when I was persecuted by the whole world, she alone was true to me.'"

Thalia stopped short, blushing like one caught in the act of making a speech. To hide her confusion, she snatched a shoe-buttoner and began trying to unlock a trunk with it.

"Go on, Thalia," I said to the flushed young speaker. "Be sure you have one sympathetic listener."

"It is nothing; only to the last the banner over her was love. Kadijah had no rival, though she was skinny and wrinkled and sunburnt. You know what horrid old witches Arabian women are after thirty."

Thalia seated herself on the low ship-trunk, much as to say, "I am through now."

The gentle Armenian seemed amused at the debate, in which she took no part. Like many another of the so-called sterner sex, it was most interesting to the debaters; but she lent a kindly ear. A woman of large experience, graceful culture, and broad, catholic spirit. "Let us hear from Armenia," said the Advanced Thinker, naturally lowering her tone into softness as she addressed the silent matron, to whom a noisy argument was a fresh novelty.

"You make a mistake," she observed quietly, in a modest way, highly contrasting with the assertive sentences just heard, "to suppose the Harem is a mere boudoir and bower, the Oriental wife the plaything of idle hours, living in butterfly idleness. In that consecrated place are all the women of the household. There lives the mother, in Eastern countries treated with the utmost delicacy and reverence. The children are there, proudly welcomed into life and tenderly reared. Slavery here is not the dreadful bondage you used to have in America. The girls you saw to-day sit with their mistress in the afternoon, and sew and talk with her in a patriarchal way you know nothing of. The Harem, the Forbidden Room, is the golden milestone, the centre of existence to the home-keeping Oriental, and, as such, has a hold controlling every action he meditates. He is deeply religious, and appeals to his mother for advice long as she lives. The women enter into every detail of the public life of their husbands, and are recognized as a power in the most difficult political affairs, as they are not even in fair France."

"Do you mean to say," asked the Advanced Thinker, amazedly, "that in time the tender little parasite we saw to-day may come to know something of grave matters of state, and be capable of advising in them?"

"I do. There are wide possibilities in that gentle soul, whose face is forbidden to the thoughts and eyes of all men but one. To borrow the words of a Christian missionary of Scutari, 'Any one who has a private scheme to advance, a policy to develop, an office to gain or to keep, a boy to provide for, or an enemy to crush, sends his wife to the harem of a grandee. Women here bring about the most astounding results. All a Moslem's spare time and money are given to adorning the 'reserved place' where *he* is the sole male communication with the outer world, and no other living man enters the screened portal without his leave. Even an officer of justice dares not set foot there, and ancient usage respects a man's seclusion in the harem to the degree that messengers wait and despatches are unopened while the master's shoes are in sight before the guarded door.'"

"These are new ideas to us," said the Advanced Thinker, meekly and in a subdued manner quite mortifying to see.

"I testify to what I have seen," said the Armenian, with her rare smile. "The tents of the Arab women are sacred places, a halt in a restless, roving life, where the man, incurably wild, turns for rest and quiet. I, *moi qui vous parle*, have seen that no people are so kind to children as the Bedouins are. They never scold or strike them; the son of a sheik is nursed and petted in the chief's tent all day long; and, in more than one tribe, it is in the women's tents that the politics are settled. You know there is a vein of poetry in even the lowest of the tribes, and the Arab calls his wife the keeper of his soul, -- a pet name, sweet and strong. Depend upon it," added the gentle lady, more positively, "women of the East have their influence and authority, not maintained in the same way, but held quite equal to the power of the women of the West."

Thalia gave the Armenian a grateful glance. "Thank you for righting us on the woman question in this latitude, where soft voices and gracious manners are the rule and seem to come by inheritance, instead of teaching."

Here the Advanced Thinker started up, and charmed our sleepy ears with one of her keen and sparkling home speeches. She is a wise woman, and you, my beloved, have probably heard her in the lecture-room and agreed with her.

Let me not weary you with the conversation, which lasted far into the night, and set us to thinking there might possibly be slight flaws in our boasted social science and polished civilization. In the solitude of my own room I pondered the subject alone. Looking out, for a good-night to the stars, throbbing white in the steel-blue sky, by a strange association of ideas I recalled a sentence of Thackeray, which has clung to memory through many changes: "We are Turks with the affections of our women, and have made them subscribe to our doctrine too. We let their bodies go abroad liberally enough, with smiles and ringlets and pink bonnets to disguise them, instead of veils and yasmaks; but their souls must be seen by only one man: and they obey not unwillingly, and consent to remain at home as our slaves, ministering to us and doing drudgery for us."

The spirit of peace brooded the waters; the winds were whist, the waves were still. A pale glimmer in the east heralded the coming day. Sirius was in the zenith, the brightest thing in the universe of God; the morning stars were out; the setting moon hung low on the horizon's edge.

Good-night to the lights above, and to the Light of the Harem, as well. Again I unclasped the miniature and gazed on the faultless picture. A cherub face, without the cherub's chubby squareness of outline; eyes soft as those of her own gazelle, as winsome, as artless, but not so sad; rather the smiling eyes of Mona Lisa, before which we wait, thinking in another moment the parted lips will say "Good-morning." The Aladdin lamp was dying, and I thought a blessing on the sunny head and spotless soul which had never known sorrow or strife.

Suppose I *could*, would I have the heart to reduce her to our prosaic and wearing level in the hard, familiar ruts; to give the king's darling a taste of the bitter fruit from the tree of knowledge?

Would you, dear reader?

XI. BYRON

IN the old Protestant cemetery at Rome, hard by the Pyramid of Caius Curtius, is the grave of Keats. His epitaph -- "Here lies one whose name was writ in water"-- was the dying wail of a broken heart. In that hour his fame appeared the dream of a sleeper, a message dropped into darkness; and among the gathering shadows of death he beheld, in prophetic vision, the dread phantom Oblivion.

He is one of the many poets whose illustrious names appear in the wavy lines of the Storied Sea. They are not transient records, and Byron disputes the ancient supremacy of Homer. His spirit walks abroad in the moonlight, in the starlight, from the Pillars of Hercules to the home of the obscene Harpies, where the Black Sea dashes against the Cyanean rocks. On that mighty tablet the name of Childe Harold is written, and over it the years have no power. At the distance of more than half a century, along the Lido of Venice, the guide points the favorite road where at evening galloped the reckless rider, whose fever of heart and brain no touch of cooling hand or balmy airs could quiet. Among the violet vales and orange groves which skirt the Bay of Naples, the cicerone tells of

"Meelor Beeron;" in the hotel, the room "Meelor Beeron" occupied is noted, mentioned, and shown, with the candlestick he carried to his unquiet bedroom. At Sphactera, which they tell you is Medora's Isle, you are shown the grotto in which the pirate chief anchored his ship: --

"HOW GLORIOUSLY HER GALLANT COURSE SHE GOES!
HER WHITE WINGS FLYING -- NEVER FROM HER FOES --
SHE WALKS THE WATERS LIKE A THING OF LIFE,
AND SEEMS TO DARE THE ELEMENTS TO STRIFE."

He has made the Aegean his own, where burning Sappho loved and sung; Coron's bay, where floated many a galley light; and, passing the Dardanelles, the captain of the "Fleur de Luce" says nothing of Hero and Leander, but, "This is where Byron swam across, three miles, in an hour and ten minutes." By the blue rushing of the arrowy Rhone and where Lake Leman lies by Chillon's walls, the waters are forever associated with the most illustrious Englishman of the nineteenth century.

At Marathon we do not recall the flying hosts of Persia; but

"THE MOUNTAINS LOOK ON MARATHON,
AND MARATHON LOOKS ON THE SEA."

The earliest and the latest singers have tuned their harps here; but his name leads all, proudest of the shining host written in the water of the halcyon sea which softly beats on the shores of that Greece to which he gave his sword, his fortune, and his life.

At Missolonghi the name of Byron is an undying memory, and last year his statue was there unveiled, with music of trumpet and bugle and national airs by martial bands. A funeral service was performed, and the clergy and civic authorities, headed by trumpeters, walked in solemn, stately procession to the site of the statue. The *préfet* said, in a voice loud enough for the crowd to hear: "Let the veil fall! Let us uncover the statue of the grand martyr of our holy revolution! the grand benefactor of Greece!"

This almost atones for the absence of his monument in Westminster, and not till I visited the East did I realize how secure is his fame.

He wrote, "Athens holds my heart and soul." The wanderer, outlawed by public opinion from his native country, turned for adoption to the classic land whose sons in desperate revolution battled for a restoration of the glories of the ancient republic. That subject should not be touched with an every-day pen, nor the land described in common phrase.

My reader of the outgoing generation may remember something of "Contarini Fleming," the most romantic, and therefore most charming to the young, of all Disraeli's romances. More years ago than I care to record, it fascinated me, and one passage from its brilliant pages has never faded from the chronicles of memory. I gladly efface my own weak effort at description for a paragraph which gives the very soul of the glorious land on the Aegean shore: --

"A COUNTRY OF PROMONTORIES AND GULFS AND ISLANDS CLUSTERING IN AN AZURE SEA; A COUNTRY OF WOODED VALES AND PURPLE MOUNTAINS, WHEREIN THE CITIES ARE BUILT ON PLAINS COVERED WITH OLIVE WOODS AND AT THE BASE OF AN ACROPOLIS CROWNED WITH A TEMPLE OR A TOWER. AND THERE ARE QUARRIES OF WHITE MARBLE, AND VINES, AND MUCH WILD HONEY. AND WHEREVER YOU MOVE IS SOME FAIR AND ELEGANT MEMORIAL OF THE POETIC PAST; A LONE PILLAR ON THE GREEN AND SILENT PLAIN, ONCE ECHOING WITH TRIUMPHANT SHOUTS OF SACRED GAMES, THE TOMB OF A HERO OR THE FANE OF A GOD. CLEAR IS THE SKY AND FRAGRANT IS THE AIR, AND AT ALL SEASONS THE MAGICAL SCENERY OF THIS LAND IS COLORED WITH THAT MELLOW TINT AND INVESTED WITH THAT PENSIVE CHARACTER WHICH IN OTHER COUNTRIES WE CONCEIVE TO BE

Byron called the subtle, quick-witted Greeks the Eastern Irish, -- an idea echoed by English statesmen of to-day. Speaking of the desperate tangle known as the Eastern Question, knotted by Epirotes of Smyrna, they say thirty Irelands are in Asia Minor.

He wrote: "They are plausible rascals. I came here expecting to find Plutarch's men. I find the morals of Newgate are better." Of Marathon, the name which makes us all Grecians, he writes: "The Plain of Marathon was offered me for the sum of nine hundred pounds. Alas! was the dust of Miltiades worth no more? It could scarcely have fetched less if sold by weight." But no disappointment or even a worn-out frame or hopeless spirit could lead him to abandon the cause he held so dear, or could chill his affection for the birthplace of heroes.

Where, he asks, is the human being that ever conferred a benefit on Greeks or Greece? "They are to be grateful to the Turks for their fetters, and to the Franks for their broken promises and lying counsels. They are to be grateful to the artist who engraves their ruins, and the antiquary who carries them away; to the traveller whose janissary flogs them, and to the scribbler whose journal abuses them."

The Greeks had looked to his arrival as they would to the advent of the Messiah. Missolonghi was at the time a pestilential prison, -- floods on the land side and sirocco from the sea. Of its marshes he says: "The dikes of Holland, when broken down, are the deserts of Arabia for dryness in comparison." He felt he should never leave it alive, and said to his faithful Tita, "Either the Turks, the Greeks, or the climate will prevent my going back to Italy." He had, as he gloomily expressed it, an old feel, and frequently alluded to a Scotch fortune-teller, who said to him, "Beware of your thirty-seventh year."

Deep melancholy yet touches us in thinking of that death-bed, among half-wild soldiers, who rested all hope of the future on this one man. The absence of womanly care or nursing, the wretchedness and desolation of his surroundings, are in bitter contrast with the ideal minstrel of the tens of thousands who had hung entranced on his numbers and who wept at his death, though they had never seen his face.

In Smyrna it was my good fortune to become acquainted with a gentleman whose father was with Byron in his last days, and from him I learned nothing new; but it seemed freshly brought to mind by hearing the reminiscences, rather than reading them.

To his mother, the strange, unnatural mother, who never ceased to taunt him and rate him as a lame brat, and whose last illness was made fatal by a fit of rage brought on by reading her upholsterer's bill, he was indebted for a belief in lucky and unlucky days. She taught him, too, a firm faith in sorcery and necromancy and the ominous fascination of the evil eye, the *mal occhio*, for which charms and talismans are found in buried Pompeii. He was so superstitious as to refuse to take medicine till some old witch was first sent for, to exorcise the evil eye which prevented its action. His morbid gloom at times bordered on insanity, of which he lived in dread, thinking himself predisposed to it by inheritance. His variable and capricious temper made the case difficult for the physicians. To the last his face wore its habitual sarcastic expression, and the customary sneer was rarely absent from the exquisite lips. You remember Scott used to say, "Byron's face is a thing to dream of, an alabaster vase lighted from within;" nor did that beauty vanish even in the hours when he repeated "Ada, Greece," the last adieu to the land of his adoption, and the sole child of his house and heart, the child of love, though born in bitterness and nurtured in convulsion.

Before embalming the body, when the preparations were ready, the physicians paused before the Eternal Pilgrim, so young in years, so absolute by genius, who had laid down his gathered sheaves of fame in what appeared a useless sacrifice.

Said my informant, involuntarily they stood in silent admiration of the surpassing beauty of his person. The restless, scintillating gray eyes were closed, and his face wore the calm of one whose last words were: "Now I shall go to sleep." About the small, compact head the hair curled naturally, already quite gray. His sickness was so short, the body was not wasted, the skin was white and delicate, and the perfect symmetry of his hands made them like waxen models. The head was that of the Apollo; but his left foot was deformed and turned inward, the left leg was smaller and shorter than the sound one. He said an accident had misshaped his leg; but there can be no doubt that he was born club-footed. Proceeding with the autopsy, they found the lungs healthy; but the appearance of the heart was singular. "Its parietes were as collapsed and of consistence as flabby as those of persons who have died of old age." He spent his summer while it was May, and was himself one of whom he sung, --

"THERE IS AN ORDER
OF MORTALS ON THE EARTH, WHO DO BECOME
OLD IN THEIR YOUTH, AND DIE ERE MIDDLE AGE,
WITHOUT THE VIOLENCE OF WARLIKE DEATH:
SOME PERISHING OF PLEASURE, SOME OF STUDY,
SOME WORN WITH TOIL, SOME OF MERE WEARINESS,
SOME OF DISEASE, AND SOME OF INSANITY,
AND SOME OF WITHERED OR OF BROKEN HEARTS;
FOR THIS LAST IS A MALADY WHICH SLAYS

"On the 22d of April, 1824," writes an eyewitness, "in the midst of his own brigade of the troops of the Government, on the shoulders of the officers of his corps, relieved occasionally by other Greeks, the honored remains were carried to the church where lie the bodies of Marcos Bozzaris and General Norman. There we laid them down. The coffin was a rude, ill-constructed chest of wood; a black mantle served for a pall; and over it we placed a helmet and a sword, and a crown of laurel. No funeral pomp could have left the impression nor spoken the feelings of this simple ceremony. The wretchedness and desolation of the place itself; the wild, half-civilized warriors around us; their deep-felt, unaffected grief; the fond recollections; the disappointed hopes; the anxieties and sad presentiments which might be read on every countenance, -- all contributed to form a scene more moving, more truly affecting, than perhaps was ever before witnessed round the grave of a great man." An English chieftain, with Suliotes for his guards and all Greece for his mourners.

XII. CLASSIC FUNERALS

DO you remember the little song which Byron sung to a young Greek girl, thereby giving her a century of fame? A slight thing, yet to this day much affected by college boys; possibly because of the foreign line which allows opportunity for airing a few words from the Lexicon. It begins: --

"MAID OF ATHENS, ERE WE PART,
GIVE, OH! GIVE ME BACK MY HEART,"

and was addressed to the lovely daughter of the Greek lady, widow of an English vice-consul, at whose house the poet lodged. In a letter to Drury (1810) he writes: "I almost forgot to tell you I am dying for love of three Greek girls at Athens, sisters. I lived in the same house. Theresa, Mariana, Katinka, are the names of these divinities," all of them under fifteen. The story (probably a lie) runs, that, in making love to one of these goddesses, he had recourse to an act of courtship common in the East, namely, giving himself a wound across the breast with his dagger. The young Athenian, by his own account, looked on very coolly during the operation, regarding it a fit tribute to her beauty, but in no way moved to gratitude or acceptance of his love.

The Maid of Athens was eldest of three sisters, on whom the beauty of the beautiful race had descended. For many years the name of Theresa Macri was familiar to travellers. Her quiet, modest home was sought out, and details of her daily life, her classic face and gentle manner, were the themes of the tourist. The rosy wreath which Byron placed on the girlish head seems to be the main incident of an uneventful life. She married Captain Black, and, mother of many children, to the last years of a long life was one of the "sights" of the violet-crowned city.

"We were invited to Mrs. Black's funeral," writes a friend living in modern Athens, "and joined the procession not far from the English cemetery, where her grave was made. That is a pleasant spot, on the banks of the shrunken Ilissus, opposite the Stadium, near 'green Callirrhoe,' -- ancient mother of monsters, now a wasted fountain. The river of poetry, consecrated by religion, legend, and tradition, could never have been a considerable stream, only what we would call a spring branch, and in the Mississippi valley would not count at all.

"Often dry in summer, it runs through the east side of the city and is lost in the marshes of the Athenian plain; but size does not make the interest of any river, else would the Amazon be worth many a Tiber. Along the banks of this irregular and fitful stream anciently were sacred groves and flowery altars, dedicated to the Muses. Its pure and limpid waters mirrored all fair and graceful shapes,-- a lovely throng, now vanished forever, with their votive tablets and memorials.

"On a neighboring hill, Plato, the divine teacher, walked and talked with his pupils, after his return from Egypt and Sicily. Hallowed is the ground by holy and venerable shades, gracious presences invisible. Here, we fancy, the young disciples might have swum in the milk-warm river of summer, and hard by are the magnificent remains of the unfinished Temple of Jupiter, like all in Greece, lovelier in death than aught else in life.

"The sun sets behind mountains which conceal the Morea from view, and in funereal thought ethereal spirits from out the dim, shadowy past attended us; ghosts of the flying Persian hosts. Four hundred and eighty years before Christ, was fought the battle of Salamis; and on a throne of precious metals Xerxes sat in royal state, and from the high mountain yonder surveyed the contest. The brass beaks of the light ships of the agile Greek broke against the clumsy Persian galleys, and the monarch, afar and impotent, watched the slaughter of his 'Immortals' and the wrecked fleet scattered to the winds, one more triumphal wreath for Themistocles that day.

"While the train moved forward we passed peasants dancing and singing in the smooth Ionian tongue, --

'AS THE HONEY MINGLES WITH MILK,
THUS THE BLACK OF OUR EYES MINGLES WITH THE BLUE OF THINE,' --

love words joined to a melody such as shepherds might have heard in the golden ages, when the world was young and the vales of Thessaly were haunted with naiad and satyr; such as Pan might have piped in mythic times to the nymphs of Arcady, banishing grief to a far dwelling on the other side of the mountains. In the shadow of the olives idlers lounged, and on little tables rattled the dice-boxes, playing games old as the Pyramids. Visit the Elder World, if you would learn the truth that there is nothing new under the sun.

"A few light clouds floated like airy scarfs above a range of low hills which terminates in the flowery Mount Hymettus. There the Attic bees yet hum in the fragrant thyme, and, through all changes, Athens is famous for olives and Hymettus for honey. A group of peasants on the hillside made a din by striking on brazen vessels, to attract a swarm which had just left the hive. In this way, when a child, I used to 'assist' with a stick, and batter a tin pan by way of adding to the tumult which an early superstition taught was the speediest way to make bees settle. That practice has fallen into contempt with the owners of patent hives, but is still continued here, according to an immemorial fashion. The wild honey is very rich, and is, indeed, sweet as pleasant words.

"Not far away from the cemetery was once the ancient Odeum, the theatre built by Pericles for musical competitions; and devout Greeks used to say the Muses haunted the burial-place of victors in these sweet contests, and made the air tuneful with lamentations over their tombs. The roof of this temple was made of masts and yards of ships of the Persian fleet defeated at Salamis, and was modelled after the tent of Xerxes. Thus did this glorious people consecrate all that was dear and precious, and the trophies of battle were made to do gentle service in preservation of the divinest of the arts of peace.

"Hard by is the Ceramicus, sacred to ashes of heroes of war, who had separate and most honored sepulture apart from vulgar dust. Venerated were their resting-places. You remember the lofty, defiant boast: 'We know no blessing but liberty, and confess no master but the gods. If thou wouldst prove our valor, come and insult the tombs of our ancestors.'

"Here, too, near the relics of the Academy, Diogenes camped in his tub, which he never used as a wash-tub. The dirty old vagabond has his fame as a philosopher, while tens of thousands have been forgotten the latchet of whose shoes he is not worthy to unloose. He bore the slings and arrows of outrageous fortune with mortifying tranquillity, and his haughty scorn of riches was equalled only by his contempt of work; a reformer of mankind, whose ideal man, a drone and a thief, was most nearly reached in Lacedaemon. 'I have found men nowhere,' said this lazy brute; 'but I have seen children at Sparta.'

"A pale blue column of smoke against the fair horizon marks the distant volcano where Vulcan used to set up his furnaces and make the Cyclops forge the thunderbolts of Jupiter. But how can I give half the associations in a single landscape where every step is on an empire's dust? Come into the tinted mist, hear the nightingale sing, and feel the soft Circean spell of the sea, sky, and soil of Greece. Their loveliness is beyond my praise.

"Let me entreat you, in the words of Lysippus: 'Whoever does not desire to see Athens is stupid; whoever sees it without being delighted, is still more stupid; but the height of stupidity is to see it, to admire it, and to leave it.'

"Softly tempered, the tender sunlight rested on the mortal remains of the Maid of Athens. The open coffin was rested beside the grave, and the placid face, exposed, must once have been remarkably fine. The low forehead and delicate, straight nose, inclining to aquiline, were still there, and the slender hands, which were folded at rest. The expression of the mouth was peaceful, but she was worn and old. The funeral was very simple in all its appointments, and few followed to the grave the poor Widow Black, whose 'soft cheek's blooming tinge' and 'wild eyes like the roe' have been sung wherever the English language is spoken.

"She was a member of the Greek Church, and Greek priests performed the funeral service. The exquisite fineness of this atmosphere carries the penetrating voices to great distances and the procession is most solemn and picturesque. The Greek priests look as though, like the Levite, without blemish or fault and selected for beauty. The deep-set, glowing black eyes are not shaded by their stove-pipe hat with a square tile at the top; a most curious head-gear, to which a black gauze veil is often attached. Long, floating robes reach to the feet, nearly always black, though sometimes purple. Long hair, straggling on the shoulders or knotted behind, gives strange blendings to a costume which makes the wearer appear neither man nor woman; and at first glance it is a question to one unfamiliar with the country."

The seeming immortality of the ancient Grecian customs is shown in the burial ceremonials; and their rich and musical language is well adapted to the wailing chants of priests, called by them Meyriology, or hymns of the dead. The absorbing interest attached of old to a funeral, and indeed every event connected with death, still adheres to the Hellenic mind. Modern religions have influenced the national language and traditions; but there is enough left of the classic rites, old as superstition, to remind one of the "Iliad" and the "Odyssey." Men let their beards grow, and women cut off their hair at the death of their husbands and bury the long tresses with them, pledges of grief and affection. There are many portions of Asia Minor where this is the common practice.

The wedding wreath of the bride is carefully laid away for the funeral, and in Epirus, so strict is custom, a widow would be despised if she contracted a second marriage. Instead of the ancient libations of oil and wine to the heathen deities, platters of sweets are left on the grave, which are appropriated by the priests.

When the last hour approaches and the last enemy is to be met, a priest is sent for and sacrament is administered. The nearest relative must come and catch the latest breath -- the parting soul -- of the beloved, give the farewell kiss, and press the dull eyelids down over the lustreless eyes. Still, as in the antique ages, do they array the corpse in holiday robes, fresh bathed, and anointed with oil and wine. It lies at full length, with crossed hands and upright feet, sprinkled with flowers, and the solemn cypress branch is hung above the door. Formerly the coffin was made of this wood. They sing, "Flowers fade, leaves wither; but the constant cypress is green forever." Friends watch the body through the night, and tapers at the head and feet are lighted. Dirges are chanted, setting forth the life and virtues of the deceased in tender valediction, and the cause of his death. These are in minor key, with long, shrill notes, that pierce the ear like the shrieks of women. The funeral usually takes place the next day after death, as in the classic years, when opinion held that not till the burial-rites are ended are the shades ferried over the fatal Styx to the Elysian Fields beyond. The soul, having left its habitation, is stopped on the banks of the black-flowing river, and wanders up and down in darkness, tormented with the desire of reaching the place of its destination. "And thus it appeared to the mourners, who should not rest till they have withdrawn the mortal relics from the eye of day and exposure to the weather."

Friends come by invitation to the house of mourning. The coffin is wreathed with flowers, if the means of the survivors afford it, or dressed with green leaves by the poorer classes. The priests assemble, and a cake, soaked in wine, is eaten by the company, who say, "O God, who gave, rest his soul." Prayers are offered, and the procession marches to the church. Crosses are carried by the clergy, and lighted tapers by the others. The coffin, opened and adorned, is borne on the shoulders of men, and black streamers, pending from it, are held by the eldest or most honored members of the cortege. When the funeral mass is ended, the priests tell the relatives to take the last farewell and leave the last kiss; then there are wailing and crying. On reaching the grave, the final prayers are offered, the coffin-lid nailed down, and the body is lowered in a shallow grave. The leading, or perhaps I might say the ranking, priest throws in a spadeful of gravel in the form of a cross, and passes the spade to the nearest of kin, who do the same in turns, repeating, "God rest his soul." The bier is then covered with the pall of black and the grave filled. Returning to the house of mourning, the invited guests wash their hands and partake of a lunch, at which fish, eggs, and vegetables alone are eaten, -- the weak modern substitute for those tremendous feasts of old, where heroes banqueted for days on the funeral-baked meats and drank the red wine, which warmed their heart's core. But those were the heroic ages, and offerings at the shrine of the mighty were in keeping with the prowess of the deceased.

At evening of the third, ninth, twentieth days masses are said for the soul of the departed, and on the fortieth day the friends assemble at the house of mourning, and, after a simple meal, proceed to the newly made grave and set up a tombstone. On the fortieth day a list of the ancestors of the dead is read and prayer is offered for their souls. It would seem the Greek faith trusts the power of prayer generations after the spirit has passed beyond the veil, and, as some Christians believe, been admitted to Paradise.

At intervals of three years these rites are observed in loving anniversaries. At the end of that time a most singular and revolting custom obtains in some provinces of the East. The tomb is opened, and if the remains are well decomposed the bones are gathered into a cloth, and carried in a basket covered with a rich garment to the church. Flowers are laid on the top and the whole deposit is left nine days, while every evening relatives go to say prayers, and the body is then reinterred.

This hideous practice, enough to corrupt the air and breed pestilence, has happily fallen into disuse. It probably originated in some remote period, when a hurried burial obliged a reinterment, and is continued in the spirit of the Boeotians. When questioned why they offered eels to the gods: "We observe the customs of our forefathers, without thinking ourselves obliged to give a reason for them." Conform to the received religion of your country, was the command of the Delphic oracle, and the well-disciplined Greeks accept the usages of the past without question, in reverence and submission which are a puzzle and a mystery to the Yankee intellect. It is excusable in a people whose history is in the past and the future, but not in the restless race working in the busy present to make history.

XIII. THE AMERICAN GIRL: AN INTERLUDE - PART I

ON a day of ennui she came aboard, and we knew her before she reached the steamer. No other girl wears a white necktie so high over the full, soft throat; no other travels in navy-blue silk, with solitaire earrings, not vulgarly large, but of pure water and fine setting; no other girl is so freshly gloved and *chaussé* (the word "booted" is too harsh for those delicate feet); and none other could or would so lightly mount the gangway, walk straight to us, and say, "We are country-women, are we not? Then let us be friends at once." How did she identify the two ladies in black, I should like to know?

A miniature woman, impossible anywhere on earth except in our land of fierce, cold, and vivid sunshine; a lithe, pliant figure, of perfect shape, from the Arab arch of her foot to the small, compact head, well set on the sloping shoulders.

After living some months among demure, suppressed European girls, much alike as rows of pins, who would regard as something dangerous and revolutionary the young republican from "the land of the free and the home of the brave," this fairy came without question into our homesick hearts.

It must be confessed she was rather conspicuous. The fineness of her toilet was noticeable, and on her arm was a Roman shawl, or rather scarf, -- rainbow stripes on black ground, -- which harmonized well with the fresh young face; but elegant silken fabrics are not often used as travelling wraps on the Mediterranean. She smiled as she touched my hand, bringing out two sets of dimples, one in each cheek, where the old war of the roses went on, and one below the long lower eyelashes. It flashed over her face like sunlight, and kindled the luminous eyes, which were neither gray, blue, nor brown, -- a mixture of these colors and better than either. We all at one moment unanimously fell in love with her, except the Antiquary. He had taken fright at her first appearance. "A pert boarding-school girl!" he said, with a sound between a snort and a groan, and fortified himself between the wheelhouse and the guard, under a large umbrella; as though she knew or cared, if she had known, what he thought.

She was attended by a tall, gawky countryman, who persisted in clutching with firm grip his own valise, in spite of persistent endeavors of the *garçon*. He was well dressed, but not able to carry off his tailoring, and was plainly oppressed by its superior make and finish, to quote the aesthetic and autocratic Devlin. The slouch hat, which identifies the native American from afar, was borne in a knotty hand, the hand of a ploughman, exposing a thick shock of hair, the color of a Maltese cat. The breeze played softly with his shaggy locks, and the rugged face was anxious, -- or was it only bored?

He seated himself on a stool near us, absorbed in gazing at the small lady he attended, though, in obedience to a signal from her, he shook hands in sober, decorous, pump-handle fashion, smiled a bony smile, and replaced the slouch between his knees. It is an established historic fact that our countrymen are a hat-wearing race, attached to their head-covering beyond all peoples, except, perhaps, the fez-wearers, who remove their national cap only in the seclusion of the harem; whereas ours occasionally uncover at meals. What was this giddy Western traveller thinking of, when he thus bared the black, bushy locks, cooled with a gray frost, to the light of common day?

"Now," said the new-comer, easily and pleasantly, as though we had known her for years, "let us tell our stories, like travellers in the story-books. The oldest first." This chapter would be entirely too long for even the gentlest of readers, did we record the facts we gave to our young friend; and then she took the word. "My name is Regina Atwood. Nina is my pet name. Papa and Mamma (emphasis on the first syllable) "died when I was little -- you are laughing at me -- when I was only so high." She held her hand about two feet from the floor. "This is my adopted father, my uncle. I have lived at school in a college town; never was away from home till the Centennial. Last year I had typhoid fever, and my hair came out. Look!" She took off her hat, with streaming plume, and threw it on the bench, baring a head of short, close curls. "I don't like these curls; they make me look so babyish. I lost my memory, and sometimes it fails me yet. We are travelling for my health. Are to summer in the Alps and winter in Egypt."

"Beware of the icy winds of the Apennines and of Rome."

"Yes, they are excavating, turning up the ancient plagues in Rome. The old gentleman yonder, camped under the umbrella, I don't know why, for it neither rains nor shines -- "

"Don't speak so loud."

"Well, then, the blooming youth in the green goggles, does he belong to your party? He looks -- what was the word we used to use in composition?" She put a finger-tip to her forehead. "Didactic! That's it. Didactic! Good to learn from, but not happy to live with."

"What a pretty hat!" said Thalia, turning the little turban on her fist, as she struck the congenial topic which makes the world of womankind akin. "Paris?"

"No, indeed. I made it myself, from scraps left of my dress. If ever I have to make a living, I shall not teach in the horrid schools, but shall open a milliner's shop. That feather used to be white. I had it dyed blue."

"Set me down as your first customer, Mademoiselle Atwood."

"Yes, thank you." And, looking at my bonnet with a dash of mischief, which dimpled her variable face all over, she added, "Suppose we begin now."

"Really, you don't mean to insinuate this London purchase is not the proper thing."

"But I do, though. That Alsatian bow is as old as the hills." And, before I knew what the little witch was about, she had whisked off the offending bonnet, had thrown a hood on my head, was blowing cinders from the bows, turning ribbons this way and that in dainty fingers, where I marked a single golden circlet. "There, now, that is something less -- less archaic, as your friend yonder might say. Uncle, the handbag, please." The relative thus accosted had the eyes of a bloodhound, and when bidden to this slight service his air was that of a faithful dog when allowed to carry its master's pocket-handkerchief. She drew from the satchel a copy of "Lucille," an old volume of Shakespeare, and a hand-glass. "Now, look," she said, "at my improvements."

"I do not care to look in the glass."

"But you must," she insisted, with a pretty, wilful absurdity, kneeling before me and holding up the mirror. "See! If poor Mamma had lived she might have been like you." Her varying face changed painfully.

"You need her, poor child; never more than now."

"So every one tells me; and I know it, for there is always something wanting, -- wanting. But," she continued, brightening up again, "I have Uncle, you see. Dear Uncle, he has been my playmate always. Everybody said we should go with the Cook's Tourists, for company, -- the Cookies we call them; but he said no. We get on better alone, and I do not care how we go, so we do go. We meet such nice people at every turn. Can't get away from them if we try."

There was an Oxford student aboard, with whom we had been friendly, -- a callow youth, in pinfeathery mustache, -- one of those brisk, dapper little men, reminders of Bantam chickens, to whom the third and fourth vowels make the "Niagara chord" that goes sounding through their lives eternally. He had the Dundreary skip, lisp, the Dundreary eyeglass, (alas! poor Yorick!) and through the pane in his eye, as our wit named it, he surveyed the quicksilvery creature as he might a dodo, or a cassowary or a specimen kangaroo from his own Australia.

He came near, and I formally presented him to the lovely, chattering maiden, and he plunged with languid movement into that subject on which, says Byron, all are fluent and none agreeable, -- self. She listened in an attitude of easy indifference, and when the platitudes ended, appeared unconscious of the existence of the autobiographer.

Thalia said, after a minute's silence: "You live in a college town. No need to ask if you have troops of admirers."

"Tribes," said Nina, unconcernedly, as one might say, "That is a grasshopper region." "Would you like to see the photographs of the Senior Class of last year? And the Faculty, too?"

"Never mind the Faculty. Bring the young gentlemen."

"Good taste on your part," she said quickly. "Those bald old men are so didactic." She put on the blue hat, and, followed by Uncle (I never learned his name), who watched like a faithful hound, she disappeared below, and quickly returned with a velvet case, full of card pictures. Then she cleared the bench, drew them out, and ranged them. "There they are, now, like four and twenty blackbirds all in a row."

"Tell their stories to us, won't you?"

"Oh! I don't know family histories. Nothing about grandfathers, Darwinian or otherwise, and all that," she continued, with a frolicsome glee, pleasant as the playful gambols of a kitten. "But what I know I tell. Now the panorama moves. Here is the aesthete, who thinks himself too sweet for anything. His room was tinted sea-green, with a dado and a bewitching frieze of lilies and swallows. The lilies were swallowing the birds or the birds swallowing the lilies, I never could tell which. Then he had a picture of Raphael, leaning his head on his hand (so!), framed in old-gold velvet, and under it a lamp, with curious figures, like the one Booth carries in 'Richelieu;' and he used to murmur about keeping the flame alive, and votive offerings of genius at the shrine of genius and the like."

"You did not admire him, then?"

"No. He was too, too utterly intense, -- always talking about melodies in blues and melodies in grays. His wife would die trying to keep at concert pitch with his melodies. Hollow! hollow!" She turned the weak, expressionless face to the wall.

"Now, here is number two, the ambitious youth, a candidate for fame, about to rush from the college campus into the arena of action."

I looked at the boyish picture.

"A plain face; but strong."

"Precisely. A good, ugly, hard worker, who took the first prizes, -- in fact, all the prizes."

"You admired him?"

"Not at all," said the little maid, wilfully, yet in a fresh-hearted, unspoiled way.

"Very young, wasn't he, to graduate?"

"No, not very, he will vote at the November elections."

The Antiquary, who had the impression he was missing something good, had folded his tent and silently stolen up to look at the picturer. We smiled at the different idea of youth she had from her listeners, feeling the sad longing of winter for spring. With a charming animation, she went on.

"Here is the athlete, in base-ball costume. You see! All muscle. In choosing for the German, we could always pick out those stumpy fingers above the screen. And here are the Cherubs, posed like the Sistine Madonna, rolling up their eyes at nothing. We called them the twins; but they were no kin. And this is the artist. He painted the regulation stork on the long panel; a view of Lake George and the Prison of Chillon; a portrait of himself, with flowing hair and a long gown."

"Yours, too, perhaps."

She nodded.

"A frightful thing! Looked like a dissolving view, as bad in its way as his marine efforts on clam shells. His studio was a chamber of horrors; and then he was forever talking of inspirations, and that Art was his bride and he would woo no other, for it sufficeth him. A do-less fellow, who will probably end as a sign-painter and call it Pompeian fresco."

"Here is number nine. He looks pale, even in a photograph. Like Hamlet, 'Man delights not me; no, nor woman neither.' He died of consumption; overwork they said. The Shakespeare Club went in a body to the funeral. He was the oldest one of the class. They called him Nestor, as though he dated back to the days of Methuselah."

"How old was he, anyhow?"

"Twenty-eight. It is pretty old, you understand." Again her audience smiled to each other.

"Here is the handsomest student in Camden College." She passed the picture round to the listening group.

"A very fine face," said one.

"Very. It was such a shame he should be so poor. Was sexton, and the boys used to call him professor of dust and ashes. Expects to go as missionary to Honolulu. The strangest part of it is, he was the poet of the class. His speech Commencement was in Spenserian verse. A splendid thing. He is very different from the artist there, in love with himself, who is so dreamy and willowy. His wife will have to support him. A masculine ivy clinging to some half-way oak, I suppose."

"You liked the poet, eh?"

"I admired him," she said; "but he was too lofty for me. See that!" She handed a lank young man in turn-down collar and flying cravat. "He gives the whole of his mind to his necktie. John Crain by name. Just look at that silly ring on his thumb. He is a howling swell -- "

"Slang from a college town?"

"Yes. I must use a little now and then. He -- " Just there a sudden gust caught the cards. We scrambled for them; but one went overboard.

"Look for a storm to-night," said Antiquary; "there is a howling swell in the sea." And, after the manner of men who rarely indulge in a witticism, he dropped his prim manner and beamed with delight at his own smartness.

"Capital!" said the maiden, graciously, with a sunny glance that would have melted a harder heart.

The punster lifted an embroidered India cap, that made him look like a scarecrow, and bowed his thanks. She held the cards tightly in her hand; and as the photograph of the Senior with a ring on his thumb floated off on the turquoise blue water, she waved them at it.

"Good-by. Good-by, John Crain. Give my love to the nymphs and the naiads, down in the corals and amber; most of all to Undine, and tell her I love her, I love her."

"But I must get on with my gallery of illustrious men," she continued gayly. "Here is the heavy German scholar. Blonde, studies late at night, and never goes to church." She handed the portrait to the Oxford bantam, whose feathers rose while he surveyed it as from a prodigious height (say the Ghizeh Pyramid) through the Cyclopean glass.

"Suppose aw -- aw foreigner like this should address aw -- aw lady like -- like aw -- "

"Like that?" said Nina, archly, holding up her own childish face on a card.

"Yes, exactly. Like that. What aw -- what would the aw -- the lady say?"

His manner was not rude, but the words meant more than met the ear. She looked steadily at him with those frank, fearless dark eyes. "I suppose she would probably smile, and say, 'Thank you; but I cannot think of marrying a man disqualified by law from holding the office of President of the United States.'"

It was as neat a stab as any Italian woman ever gave with the silver stiletto which serves her for a hair-pin. The Oxford man looked at her in a dazed, bewildered way. She was cool as snow and moonlight. Then he slipped out of sight.

"My little countrywoman, you take your fate *dans vos deux mains*, as our French cousins say."

"Oh! I didn't mean anything," she said innocently, and chatted on indifferent, as though Oxford had swung off on one of the rings of Saturn. If it was acting, it was perfect. I did not know. I never knew if it was more or less than that; but she never brushed away a gnat with less concern.

"You have had enough for to-day," she said, with sudden variation of expression, which gave the final charm to her evanescent beauty. "Run over the rest, and I will put them up."

I glanced at the remaining cards and counted them.

"Here they are. Twenty-one, twenty-two; you said there were twenty-four. Where is twenty-four?"

"Yes, one went overboard." She hesitated at a temptation to tell a fib, and affected to search among the shawls for the missing Senior. Involuntarily she put her hand to her bosom. A strong bound of the heart it was which sent the upspringing flash of scarlet flame into her cheek. Ah! little one, the secret was out. I, too, have dwelt in Arcadia, and know what was at the end of the Venetian chain clasped round the white neck, with vows and promises and never-ending kisses. In that soft resting-place, "a thing to dream of, not to tell," over the heart which beat so fast, was hidden the portrait of the missing Senior. The burning blush passed, leaving a hot, red spot in her cheek, and a fluttered nervousness took possession of her. The white hand trembled like a tendril in the breeze, as she stooped, pretending to button her shoe; but she could not hide the flush which reached to the kinky curls at the back of her neck.

"Now I must look after Uncle's bangs," she said in a merry voice, and, turning where her guardian sat, she began to smooth his gray locks with love-pats, now and then hitting him a little tap under the chin with the back of the brush to make him hold his head up. A thousand careless graces waited on her steps; not the rich gift of beauty only, but witching ways not to be described, -- a force resistless as the airy kiss of the first fragrant breeze of spring. You open your window and your heart; you turn your face to it, and would kiss it back again, if you could.

As for Uncle, at first I took him for a well-meaning idiot; but, finding a gleam of intelligence in his peculiar face, gave him the benefit of a doubt, and made him a patient study. After all, there is nothing so interesting as humanity, and I discovered a case not named in the lists of medical works; one where the heart had absorbed the brain and there was thought of only one object. Easy to see there were but two places in the world for him, -- where she was and where she was not. To be near was all the dumb worshipper asked or wished; and with his idol was supreme content. It radiated from the strange eyes, so fierce at times, and again, when bent on her, so fond. I have seen that rapt, ecstatic look in the shining morning face of young lovers, in the mother when she feels for the first time her first-born's breath; but only in this instance have I known it on the face of a person of mature years.

He closed his eyes, and she told him he looked too sweet for anything; whereat the doting Uncle smiled such an inane smile I do believe he believed every word she said. The hair-dressing ended, she seated herself in his lap, in defiance of the prejudices of civilization, -- our refined and polished civilization, which allows our daughters, those fresh and virgin blossoms, to go whirling and whirling in the coarse clasp of a *blasé* man of the world, to the swell of voluptuous music, the dreamy waltzes of Strauss, panting arm in arm to the last stretch of nerve and muscle, not infrequently coming down in a heap on slippery floors, and dropping, at last, exhausted on a sofa.

XIV. THE AMERICAN GIRL: AN INTERLUDE – PART II

AFTER the Senior Exhibition the wind freshened, and I staggered down below to lie with shut eyes and set teeth and wrestle with the enemy. Thinking of the blessed land was interrupted by the careful opening of the door, and into the darkened room came Nina Atwood, with a small bowl in her hand. She was lithe as a panther, and her tread was soundless as snow on snow.

"Lift your head," she said, with the air of a dictator.

"I have no wish to lift my head."

"But you must. Here is beef tea. I told the stewardess, in choice Ollendorff, how to have it made after our own cooking-club receipt, with just one ring of onion in, to give a home flavor. Come, come."

Philosophers say, where there is strength to command there is always obedience. This uncrowned queen, well named Regina, -- I could no more resist her than you could. I took the bowl, gulped down the dose, failing, however, to detect the home flavor. "Your health and mine, my Hebe. It was most kind, and I thank you heartily."

"Not at all. Now, mind, no more ice, but beef tea, boiling hot, -- that's what you want. Don't speak another word." And she stole out. A minute later, she was arguing with Uncle against locking her in her stateroom and keeping the key. "Suppose," she pleaded, "there should be fire, and I locked in. Dreadful!"

"I should be by you, honey, long afore you smelt smoke," said Uncle.

She could twist him round her little finger in sovereign sway till it came to guarding her. There the old man was unbending as the ancient emperor who sealed his edicts with the hilt of his sword.

The most amazing thing about seasickness is that the instant it leaves you are absolutely well and the misery forgotten. After the life-giving draught of beef-tea, with a ring of onion in it, the patient fell asleep, and, waking in the dusk, found the vessel steady.

"That child on deck! What is she doing now, Thalia?"

"She is sitting in the old arm-chair called Uncle, still as a mouse, twirling the ring on her left hand."

"Thinking of the twenty-fourth Senior."

"No doubt. She is still as still can be. An angel not much disguised."

"And the night?"

"A Mohammedan night. The scent of Paradise."

We went on deck. In the solemn beauty of the afterglow the sea lay in halcyon repose; only a vague unrest, soft as the stir of silken wings, ruffled the surface of the water. The lull of the tranquil evening shed a calming influence on the passengers of the "Fleur de Luce." The gentlemen smoked, the Roman priest fumbled his beads, the chattering Frenchmen were still. Among the august and glorious stars Orion moved in shining armor, and the Pleiades watched serenely, as they used to watch the wandering Ulysses.

We could almost hear the sirens singing on their coral isles, where they lie among beds of scarlet poppies and golden asphodel. In the dimness fairy shapes were floating, and beckoning hands stretched out to us in the shadowy distances.

"Can you give us a song, my little girl?" I asked.

"With pleasure. I can sing best standing," she said, rising from the old arm-chair. "There are but two subjects for song, -- love and death; which shall it be?"

"Love, by all means."

"You shall have one of love and death both."

Then, without apology or hesitation, she began "The Maid of Dundee" in a voice of slender sweetness. It was clear as a bobolink's, and showed careful training. You know that hackneyed ballad. It had a fresh charm in the birdlike notes, floating in the placid air of the Storied Sea. When the lines

"'O GOD,' SHE CRIED, 'LET ME GO TOO,
AND BE WITH MY JAMIE, SO GOOD AND TRUE,'"

died into silence, I watched a Swiss gentleman in the dry mediaeval epoch wipe his eyes. In that tender idyl of a simple life did he hear far away flutings under summer windows? Did thoughts long buried rise out of their graves, like gentle ghosts, haunting the gates of an Eden forever lost, there where Junes and roses bloom, and the nightingale is always singing in the green stillness of a shady garden?

My reader who possesses the vision and faculty divine may read the hearts of men and women, and look below the surface currents, to depths where the treasures lie; but I cannot tell, who am neither prophet nor seer.

Walter Scott said that there is romance enough in every life for a three-volumed novel; and we may be sure the Swiss gentleman had his, and a lost love, which the pensive strain brought back from among flowers long withered and dear faces nothing now but dust.

"If we had a guitar," said Nina, "it would be something to lean on, so we could sing together."

The guitar was brought. "It was left by a poor Neapolitan, who died aboard," said the Captain. Two of the strings were broken; but the singer pieced them together in the luminous dusk, declining the help of a lantern's light. "I leave it below concert pitch, to make it easy for the strings and the singers; and after a story we will try it."

The story-teller gave the Crimean War. Rather a modern tale for one fond of hoary antiquities. I suspect it was mainly to recite the "Charge of the Light Brigade," which he did with fine spirit, and told the death of poor Nolan of the valiant heart, and how, the night before the assault on the Malakoff, the soldiers in the English camp sang by hundreds along the line, --

"SONG OF LOVE AND NOT OF FAME;
FORGOT WAS BRITAIN'S GLORY.
EACH HEART RECALLED A DIFFERENT NAME,
YET ALL SANG, 'ANNIE LAURIE.'"

After that we sang with guitar accompaniment "Annie Laurie," Uncle bearing along that singular part known to ancient New Englanders as "Counter." Then came the "Star-spangled Banner;" "The Marseillaise," out of compliment to the Captain; and "John Brown's Body," with a rousing chorus. So pleased were we that we rapturously applauded ourselves, and treated the audience to generous encores. The prettiest thing was a Spanish song of Nina's about the Rose of the Alhambra drooping of loss for a Crusader dying before his return from Palestine. Here the guitar-strings snapped, and we had to give it up.

What pride Uncle took in his treasure, hovering about her with a homely chivalry, watching every movement, and coming in on old "John Brown" with a booming bass! And, to tell the whole truth, we all doted on the light-hearted, lovable girl, so full of winsome ways, with gentle fearlessness going through the world unconscious that it held anything less innocent than herself.

To me she was like some rich, sweet reminiscence of a life from which the morning light has vanished. I warmed with her sunny warmth, and tasted a little sip of her brimming cup of happiness that overflowed all it touched. Then she looked so fragile, -- the look which the travelled reader, for whom I do *not* write, may have seen in the faces of Grenze's pictures. My heart reached after her in a way known only to mothers, and not to all mothers, as I noted the difference between this refined "rose red" clay and the stuff of which the shaggy Uncle was made.

We lingered, sorry to part, till the calm evening glided into midnight. When the little boat came alongside, next morning, Nina said she was sorry; but then they were going to Verona, and she should see the House of the Capulets, and the tomb of Juliet, and was sure we would meet again. The light cradle bowed and courtesied good-by, and she made a pennon of the Roman scarf tied to Uncle's umbrella. The end dipping into the water, she caught it up; and as the striped streamer filled with wind, she sat under it in the shimmer of the sea, like Iris under the heavenly arch, never spirit of sun or storm, song or fable, more lovely. So she floated from sight, and into my dreams forever.

Blessings were showered on her fair young head; the Captain waved his cap; Oxford politely uncovered his baldish pate, where time was making tracks among the blond locks; Antiquary swung his Indian turban gallantly; -- when they were lost in a gray vapor, and it was all as a dream when one awaketh.

I must not forget to mention there was a black servant aboard, in some menial capacity; a Nubian, I think. A dwarfish shape, with face so badly pitted by small-pox that it looked like a burnt waffle. Nina once caught a glimpse of the little fellow, and had sent him a small piece of gold coin. As she left the steamer, the poor boy, who looked more brute than human, knelt on the lower deck, and followed her with eager eyes, gesticulations, and grimaces that would have been laughable, had they not been painful. The language of signs is universal, and we understood it was worship of the divinity that had made him rich with gold, and her tender pity better than much fine gold. Said the Captain: "The poise and self-reliance of the American lady are the admiration of all the world who has the happiness to know her. My little daughter, of her age, is in the Convent of the Sacred Cross, among the holy sisters. I wish Mademoiselle Atwood had a maid with her."

"The girl who makes her own bonnets has not much need of any one to pick up her slippers."

"Quite right; only it looks somewhat rash to be going around in this way. Yet," he added, thoughtfully, "elle est à l'abri du mal par la purité."

"Precisely," said Antiquary, triumphantly. "She is sweet as a dream come true, and is as well guarded as the Lady in Comus."

It is doubtful if the Captain of the "Fleur de Luce" is acquainted with that divinest Lady; but he murmured, "Vraiment! vraiment!"

"Her visible guardian is enough. Uncle is no fool. He watches her like a hawk. Did you notice how he glowered at Oxford? There was an evil brightness in his eyes whenever the young gentleman approached his jewel. At the least impertinence he would think no

126

more of taking that upstart by the back of his neck and dropping him over the poop than he would of drowning a blind puppy. You would have to shoot that man to get him out of the way."

"She is on a broad and dangerous journey," said Thalia, "and I wish she had some careful woman near. But," she continued fervently and cheerfully, "we must have faith in the angels. They will carry the innocent feet safely along greater perils than the edge of Vesuvius, nor will she lose any portion of the snowy whiteness of the purity which is her best defence."

"Well, well, God bless her and her husband too. Good and brave, rich and handsome, should he be who wins that pretty hand. But women marry so strangely, what if she should throw herself away on some cold clod, giving out the whole treasure of her loving nature where she can have no return? Her heart is deep as the Danube, and she may be fated to the silent sisterhood of unknown martyrs. We know many such, you and I."

"The destinies have no such doom for her," said Thalia, warmly. "I have cast her horoscope, and see her future as in a clear glass. She will go safely home, bearing the delicious perfume of travel, as Longfellow calls it. I read in the shady leaves of Destiny that she will marry the twenty-fourth Senior, will be a blithe and busy housekeeper in some happy valley of the West, maybe a snug nest on the edge of a flowery prairie. She will be ingenious as the immortal New England housekeeper who could drive in tacks with a flat-iron and draw them out with a spoon-handle; will make cake in the morning, and go to the Shakespeare club in the evening; be foremost in the fruit and flower mission, and the author of a few papers in the St. Nicholas, catching a stray leaf from the green Isle of Palms. Though not a prophet nor a prophet's son, I foresee that Uncle will enrich her with his corn-lands; her last days will be her best days; her children will rise up and call her blessed; her husband, also, and praise her."

Thalia has latterly developed a suspicious amount of sentiment. It may be possible she is thinking of exchanging her weeds for orange blossoms.

But what ailed the day? I did not know our steamer could be so dull. Slight clouds obscured the sun, and, with quick perception of the beautiful, an Italian sailor said, "The Signorina with the shining face has taken our fair weather with her." Later, a fine, cold rain set in, and the party was very dismal. Our feeble efforts at gayety died a natural death. The gentlemen solaced themselves with cigars, and discussed the prehistoric monoliths of Palenque and Copan. Thalia fell to crochet, and I turned to you, dear reader, for rest and refreshment. The lump of ambergris which had flavored the Sultan's cup was missing.

You who are of my faith that the young American girl is the sweetest thing created since the evening and the morning were the first day, readily understand this is not an ideal sketch. The subject of it is not unknown in Baltimore. In Washington she has shed a soft light, like a rose-blush, in the Arctic Circle (sometimes called the Diplomatic); and in the little town of Athena, not a thousand miles west of Indianapolis, look in the mirror, O my darling, and behold -- a portrait.

With dire forebodings these last two papers are committed to the post. The Judicious Friend who wants accurate information condemns them as light and trifling. Oh, J. F., if you hunger and thirst after knowledge, read Buckle's "History of Civilization" and Hallam's "Middle Ages," refresh your thirsty soul with salubrious pages of Gibbon, or come home to the free banquet spread in our own "Congressional Globe;" but

as for me and mine, we do not steer for the Valley of
Dry Bones,

"AS WE SAIL, AS WE SAIL."

XV. SOMETHING ABOUT HOMER

WE were warmly invited and urged to visit the scenes of the Iliad, but did not go. Why should we? It involved tents, courier, servants, risk of catching the fever of the country, being bitten to death by mosquitoes or poisoned by bad water. It is in this classic region that the world-renowned Congress of Fleas was held. "Had they been unanimous," writes the English reporter, "they could have lifted me out of bed; but, luckily, there was a division, and I never discovered to which side I belonged."

Malaria hangs heavily over the Troad, and powerful doses of quinine are needed to save the pilgrim from the pestilence that walketh in darkness and wasteth at noonday. Not so bad as the Roman Campagna, where it is death to sleep; but surpassing the swamp lands of the Mississippi Valley in the dread month of August, when ripe vegetation is rotting and the ague hangs its yellow sign over the smitten faces in the farm-houses. I had thought some spot was happily exempt from this curse of the world; but no, even in rainless Egypt the overflow of the Nile leaves lagoons and marshes, -- lurking-places for the insidious enemy, not numbered among the ancient plagues.

We knew exactly what was to be seen in the little town, never containing over four thousand citizens, which has held a large place in the imaginations of ninety generations of men. I have been sadly *disillusioné* in many things since I used to fancy those famous walls -- which some wise men contend were made of *adobes* -- were high as the stupendous walls of Babylon, and the Scæan gate was like the brazen gates of mighty Thebes. From the deck of the "Fleur de Luce" we saw -- or fancied we could see, which was just as well -- the point of land where poor Hecuba was buried, and about a league away the promontory of Sigeum. Ambitious students climb to the top, where Achilles is buried; and there Alexander ran naked round his tomb, in honor of his manes, -- doubtless to the great comfort of that unquenchable and unresting spirit. Had we strained over scorched plain and stony roads on a back-breaking donkey, it had been to see nothing but a few slow men, digging at a leisurely rate in the poor, burnt-out soil. Priam's treasure-house has been rifled; there is no chance for finding golden relics of Paris, Helen's necklace, or Hector's spear. If such inestimable treasure from that far epoch lay there, it would not be for us, but would be caught up and appropriated before our eyes beheld it.

Had we chosen to camp near the desert hills, we might have watched in vain for the gleam of lance, shield, or helmet of flitting spectres, revealed in visions to the believing Grecian. Certain scholars, who see with eyes anointed, have been known to recognize the tall shade of Agamemnon, with gigantic stride, looming above the tumuli; and, stately and sullen, the skulking shadow of Ajax, remembering in eternity the old spites against his chief and the hate still rankling against the successful rival for the celestial armor of Achilles.

If my precious reader wants to see what the gods are doing now, he must summon buoyant courage, high hope, and robust faith, and for himself call up the ghosts out of the underworld, and with phantoms repeople the lone city of Priam.

After the destruction of Troy, a new city of the same name was built by Alexander, about thirty stadia from the ancient site. I take this fact from the guidebook, and hope you know what a stadium is. I do not.

Dr. Schliemann's experience illustrates the sustaining power of faith, even in earthly things. The doubters and scoffers are silenced by his convincing testimony, and their sneers no longer assail the wondrous tale of Troy divine. Pale shades hover about, perplexing the student with inconstant shadows; but localities are fixed. Yon strip of volcanic earth and rock is Tenedos, the station to which the Greeks withdrew their fleet, in order to induce the Trojans to believe they had sailed away and to receive the wooden horse.

And that is Imbros, lying in the azure sea. The space opposite them is the plain where the tents of the Greeks were pitched, and from which they were chased to the ships. Here the galleys and triremes unloaded the troops; and this exquisite air -- for sea and sky alone are unchangeable -- echoed the musical shouts of noisy sailors, and the thundering voices of the Trojan peers and sceptred kings of Greece, as they battled in never-ending duels. Their light boats must have had a time landing, for the winds were fitful and capricious and are yet. You remember that in one of these isles Æolus reigned, -- the monarch who showed Ulysses his twelve children, and who had dominion over the twelve winds, -- and here the wanderer received of him an ox's hide, enclosing *all the winds*, leaving free none but the friendly home wind, to play in the sails, murmur of quiet havens, and waft them gently back to Ithaca.

What dire misfortunes befell when the covetous mariners untied the precious bag, thinking it loaded with gold, when out they rushed with hissing sound, like the rush of many waters. Is it not all written in the story-books; and how the ship was driven back in one hour what it had taken nine days to track; and the remorse and despair of the men, and the noble forbearance of their chief?

The breezes have never been prisoners since then. Æolus still hunts the whirlwinds over land and sea, and they blow this way and that, making heavy seas, which in the Olympian dispensation went hard with the sailers, but do not greatly affect our steamers.

Here the fifty ships of Achilles anchored, and this is the coast-line which bounded his vision for nine years. He is the true hero of the Iliad, and carries away our whole heart with the palm of strength and grace. For he was bravest and handsomest of the bravest, handsomest race this old earth of ours has produced, and he knew well how to win favor in the eyes of beautiful women. Affectionate and tender, though he had been fed on the hearts of lions and the marrow of bears; and, when the choice was offered, preferred to die early and gloriously, rather than live a long life of inglorious ease. Reading the record among these old shadows, we easily forgive his quarrel with the king of men, when he shook his golden locks and shut himself up in his tent, refusing to take further part in the war, till roused by the voice of his mother to avenge the death of his dearest friend. And then to lie, dying, at the Scæan gate, having fought the battle only to miss the victory. There is no history half so real as this legendary and supernatural story, nor any pathos equal to the struggle where the gods took part and talked to men as friend with friend.

How weary those ten years of siege, let those tell who have had one year in the dreary monotony of a changeless camp. In every army the few fierce hours of combat bear a slight proportion to long intervals, where the dull, slow weeks drag after each other in unvarying sameness. No wonder the tenth year was one of domestic quarrels. You soldiers, who have cursed with curses loud and deep the inaction of your superior officers while you were panting for a move, or, in the classic language of the modern camp, spoiling for a fight, can best fancy the undying hates nursed in the ample leisure of ten years. With what strength the feuds grew and enlarged in each hateful day of enforced idleness! How the grudges and rankling jealousies burnt deeper and deeper, while the soul of Agamemnon, king of a hundred kings, rejoiced over the dissensions fulfilling the sacred prophecy. What storms of rage gathered and broke against rival chieftains, till in the contest for the arms of Achilles, the conquered Ajax rushed into an awful madness, slaughtering the sheep of his own army, distracted by the idea they were enemies, and ending by destroying himself.

These marvellous warriors were clansmen, carrying on the feuds of powerful nobles; and the chiefs naturally varied the vapid monotony of inaction by a watchfulness of the weak points of former foes, whom they hated more than they feared. They neither forgot nor forgave; and memories of gallant deeds gave them boundless faith in their ability to conquer wherever they chose to plant their standards.

Whoever has lived in camp can picture the weary days, like to each other as the swell and fall of the waves on this serene and silent shore. Instead of our routine of drill and discipline, the Greeks had wrestling matches, foot and chariot races, single combats, the discus, and archery and javelin exercise.

135

The little boats, with sails like the wings of swallows, and narrow keels, cutting the blue floor, are such as brought recruits from Sparta when war was not a science or the trade of a separate class, but the pastime of princes and the ultimate ambition of kings.

In their practice men had to stand up to the thrust of cold steel and the hideous scent of warm human blood, instead of the sulphurous fumes of gunpowder and balls, from remote and unseen machinery.

There was no newspaper, to relieve the leaden gloom of the ancient days; no tobacco, to solace picket duty; I doubt if the paymaster -- most cheering apparition -- appeared at his appointed seasons. No cheap novels were scattered about the tents, no letters from home, or express boxes; it is not known if they had the comfort of cards; -- nothing but their darling hates to cherish and keep warm; and how dear these may become, the veteran in no way like Themistocles may tell as he recalls those old nights when the trophies of another would not let him sleep.

The ancient beauty has not disappeared from the beautiful race, though alien blood has corrupted the pure strain, till it is no longer the rule, but the exception. When found, it is a thing to dream of. I once saw a fisher boy, or, rather, youth, on one of the Cyclades, mending his net, who had a face correct as the statue of Antinous. He was dressed in greasy tarpaulin; on his short, clustering locks a fillet of red cord gave the final picturesque touch to a perfect head. As he lifted his dreamy brown eyes to gaze on the passing stranger, so Paris might have looked on many-fountained Ida. So looked the shepherd boy by the moon's light on old Latmos, when Dian stooped to kiss him.

Did you ever think, dear reader, what deep consolation those miraculous beings descended from gods found in eating? Have you considered the charming simplicity of their banquets? When the king of men, towering above all Grecians in dignity, majesty, power, entertained in his grand pavilion, Clytemnestra was not concerned about aesthetic china and the like, nor did she look after the forks and spoons, for there were none. The leaders of the hosts of Greece and the confederate kings banqueted on beef killed, skinned, and roasted before their eyes. Pretty tough it was, too!

> "A STEER FOR SACRIFICE THE KING DESIGNED,
> OF FULL FIVE YEARS AND OF THE NOBLER KIND.
> THE VICTIM FALLS, THEY STRIP THE SMOKING HIDE,
> THE BEAST THEY QUARTER AND THE JOINTS DIVIDE,
> THEN SPREAD THE TABLES, THE REPAST PREPARE,
> EACH TAKES HIS SEAT AND EACH RECEIVES HIS SHARE.
> THE KING HIMSELF (AN HONORARY SIGN)
> BEFORE GREAT AJAX PLACED THE MIGHTY CHINE."

Imagine the godlike Ajax tearing away at the marrow bones with his dripping fingers. Heroic feasts for heroic stomachs, always ready for a square meal. Philosophers call this living near to Nature. They tell us the modern Greeks have a wonderful gift of speech-making, like their long-gone ancestors, and in their musical tongue they hand down from wrinkled age to blooming youth the misty traditions of bygone glory. They have, too, tales of the farthest East, of sorceries and witchcraft, of charms and drugs possessed with magic, genii and afrite, and hidden treasures in enchanted caverns. The legends of unknown antiquity have easy faith among them, supernatural agencies are trusted, and sailors in every sea are more or less superstitious.

An isolated life tends to nurture weird fancies, and the spinning of yarns is heard wherever wood will float. The enjoyment of the story-teller depends largely on the interest and patience of the listener, and the rare, fine talent of continuous attention is a peculiar attribute of the boatmen of the Levant. One man will tell a tale lasting through the mariner's leisure hours for a week, and the audience remains unwearied and attentive. Watching the long-protracted sessions of amusement in these times of interruption and impatience, one has the same sensation as in looking through certain books newly issued from the press; the wonder is not that they were written, but that they are ever read.

An army of imagining men, as the actors in the great epic have been well called, naturally located in Samothrace, the Holy Hill, the watch-tower of Jove the Thunderer. From that ethereal height he despatched the Twin Brothers, of matchless swiftness and silent pace, to bear away the body of Sarpedon, fair as in life and undefiled, though dragged through the dust of the crimsoned plain. In the soft arms of silent Sleep and Death they floated the young spirit home to eternal rest in the bosom of his father.

You sad mourner for the brave and the beautiful, see the rich meaning, passing the wisdom of the wise, garnered in the fanciful truths to which we give the name of fables.

We disputed about the geography of the Iliad. Who does not? But I am not disposed to get into hot water, -- like the wise counsellor, "would fain die a dry death," -- and therefore reserve argument till we meet face to face, O my beloved! We heard the surge and thunder of the Odyssey, though steering through a summer sea, and, winding among the historic isles, many times we said, "How like New Mexico!" They are arid upheavals of volcanic rock, bare reddish slopes, at torrid heat in the noonday shining. There may be verdure and bloom on the sides away from the sight, but from the deck of the "Fleur de Luce" we saw little vegetation. We had expected gardens and vineyards, bowers of roses, with birds-of-paradise and butterflies darting like winged thoughts among them, tangled vines, festoons of ivy in luxuriant verdure running wild. I had pictured pomegranate-trees with blossoms like flame glowing in a background of tender green; but we did not find them. Here and there was a tower or castle, old in story, picturesque and venerable, which had withstood strokes of stones hurled by the catapult, and scars gashed and torn by battering-rams ages before gunpowder was in some sort anticipated by Greek fire.

On those isles of barrenness and rock are sparse, straggling villages, meagre gardens of scant, starved herbage; along the dried-up streams, not a willow large enough for Homer to hang his harp on.

The winding Mæander is shrunken to a mere thread now, and the Scamander, -- "the divine Scamander," fed by springs on Ida, -- once choked with dead bodies by Achilles, would not float a single corpse now. Yet this is haunted ground, most interesting by association reaching to a hoary antiquity. Here the blind first singer wandered with footsteps set to music, and sung high, heroic measures, -- not such songs as we hear to-day from strolling minstrels, who thus make their bread. Wait till the sun sets in a sky absolved from every taint of cloud or mist, and the remotest island becomes a soft purple stain on the horizon; when the highest peak is a mount of transfiguration, an unknown heavenly land in a glory of ineffable loveliness, blent of violet, rose, and gold; -- in this tranquil hush the winds and the waves arc at their evening song, answering the wooing sirens. We forget the wrathful gods and the petty warring in the battle we call life, and deeply feel all that poets have sung and dreamers dreamed in this Kingdom of the Beautiful Myths. The thrilling sense passes with the hours, the glare of next day's noon is a disenchanter, and the dim vision of the night seems vague and unreal as the vanishing mirage of some long-gone summer morning. Still, Memory, who loses more than she treasures, will never let that heavenly picture go. The moon was at its full when we made the voyage of the Homeric Islands. That night, -- what was it but the delicate shade of a day that is dead? The white moonshine touched with silver the bright hair of Thalia, as she leaned over the guard to watch the dolphins play and hearken to the rhythmic flow of the water. The sea seemed to listen as she murmured, --

"IN SUCH A NIGHT AS THIS,
WHEN THE SWEET WIND DID GENTLY KISS THE TREES
AND THEY DID MAKE NO NOISE, -- IN SUCH A NIGHT
TROILUS, METHINKS, MOUNTED THE TROJAN WALLS,
AND SIGHED HIS SOUL TOWARD THE GRECIAN TENTS,
WHERE CRESSID LAY THAT NIGHT."

It was the voice of the poet of the past saluting the poet of all time.

XVI. ABOUT SMYRNA – PART I

THE guide-book says the early history of Smyrna is disfigured by fables. Let us rejoice that a place in American minds associated only with figs lives in the pale twilight of fable, where flickering mythic lights produce lovely effects, changing men to demigods and making heroes of common clay. I have written elsewhere, and of a very different people, that there is no myth without its teaching. Most exquisite poetry veils subtle meaning, and the old pagans well knew the deep wisdom that lay hidden in their fantasies, to which the modern unbeliever attaches no value.

Isman Giaour, or Infidel Smyrna, is one of the Amazon cities whose names have faded from history and are lost to the chronicler. My classic reader, if I am so fortunate as to have one, will remember how, toward the conclusion of the Trojan War, the Amazon queen came to the city of Priam with the gallant band of archers, and rushed on the Greeks, and how she was killed by the great-souled Achilles. It was to this city, "where the blue-haired sea shakes the land," that Circe sent for the enchanted wine by which men were transformed into swine, all except the wise Ulysses. Over him the Daughter of the Day had no witchery

141

with her sorceries, because the messenger of the gods, swift Hermes, had given him to wear the small white blossom called moly, which was a charm against every sort of magic. I love to think young eyes, not dimmed by age, tears, or study, read this paper, and so I tell the old tale of Circe once more.

She was one of a family of sorcerers, sister of Medea, and she lived in a pleasant island near the floating Isle of Æolus, named Ææa, and was wisest of all men and women. Only the superior gods were wiser. The haughty beauty was the child of the Sun. The brightness of her father's face shone in her hair, her voice was a moving music that charmed the ear and ravished the soul. She held her proud state in a palace built of precious stones and jewels, that sparkled like fire, lighting the hill on which it stood, and showing the road up which she enticed many lovers. Before the shining gate lay many animals, once wild, now made tame by her art, -- wolves gentle as lambs, lions which had forgotten their fierceness, and spotted leopards soft and playful as kittens. Hard by was a herd of swine in a disgusting sty, -- grunting, squealing, wallowing brutes, that were once brave, victorious heroes. Vainly did they entreat her pity; from that horrid spot, morning and evening, noon and midnight, went up the cry: "O Circe, give back my manhood! hear, oh, hear my prayer!" But she was deaf to entreaty. By a crystal window of the palace she sat at her loom, her long hair floating like a golden glory round her, as she spun and wove a web of mingled silver and gold, the colors of the night and day. It was a subtle fabric, finished with a skill which she had gained of the gods, and so glorious mortal eye could scarcely look upon, much less imitate it. When a strong wind would bring to her the words of the prayers of transformed wanderers, a strange light burned in the steadfast eyes of the fair witch maiden, and the magic of her glance was the surer. At times she sung, as she spun, a song of ineffable sweetness, such as drew men against their will to her feet, almost their very souls out of their bodies. When it sounded from the palace window, the clouds stood still in mid blue and listened, the trees bent their high heads and hushed the flutter of their leaves, and all animals held their breath to hear. That was her chosen moment to offer the Smyrna wine to the enraptured worshippers; and she rejoiced in reducing them to beasts most wretched, because in the metamorphose they kept their human hearts unchanged. Happier had they been doomed to wander, forlorn manes of unburied bodies, by the shores of the forgetful river and the dreaded Styx, denied by the Fates a rest in the land of Shades, condemned to flit forever along the fields of the dead.

Circe was a mighty magician; besides the power which brought the sagest of scholars to knock at her gates, she could move the moon from her sphere, make the sun turn pale, the stars whirl out of their courses, and the rocks and hills to clap their hands. She had delights and recreations "to fetch the day about from sun to sun, and rock the tedious year as in a delightful dream." She had sworn by the Styx the dread oath of the gods to bring Ulysses into her toils.

'Tis an old tale, and often told, how Ulysses, the waster of cities, learning that his companions had vanished by foul witchcraft, snatched his sword and bow, to rescue his companions from the strong spell of the great enchantress. Guided by the song of matchless charm, like the lyre of Orpheus, he sought alone the shining, lion-guarded gate, where his men lay, grunting swine. They crawled to his feet, incapable of speech, licked his hands, and by hideous noises made him understand they recognized their noble leader. How the sorceress failed in her scheme of conquest of the immortal Greek, is it not all written in the books of the Chronicles of heroes? And what are the myths but cloudy shapes through which the acts, deeds, and thoughts of olden time are floated down to us in a dim and shadowy light, all loveliness?

To ears tuned aright the siren with the drinking-cup of strong Smyrna wine is singing here yet, and the modest little herb, with the white blossom, called moly, is only the white flower of a spotless life, which none wore of old but the blameless knight Ulysses, -- he who never forgot in ten years the cliffs of rocky Ithaca, his first love, fair Penelope, and her child, waiting by the seashore for his return.

Yet the guide-book tells us Smyrna is disfigured by fables.

There were settlements on this coast when Rome was merely a group of straw-built huts on the Palatine; when Samson, blind and fettered, did grind in the prison-house of his enemies; when our British ancestors were living in caves, eating roots and dressed in shaggy skins of wild animals. There were towns of respectable size near the sea before the first of the Moguls was enthroned at Delhi. Before Alexander wept because there were no more worlds to conquer, here were hills white with temples and palaces "ribbed with colonnades" of fairest marble.

The bustle and activity of this modern Smyrna, a Greek city of 180,000 souls, overpower the gray antiquity of the place, and only by far-sighted glances do we penetrate to the beginnings of this least sluggish of all Asiatic towns. The soft Oriental repose of the East is broken at Smyrna by the wily Greeks, who may have forgotten, though we can never forget, their glorious ancestors. It is one of the seven cities claiming the birth of Homer. A cave was shown where he wrote his verses; here was anciently his temple, and here he received divine honors and medals were stamped with his name. Let us not be of the number of unbelievers who think his fame was obscured in life. There were hearers then who believed his songs excelled all that can ever be written. And at the end of the hymn to the Delian Apollo, which Thucydides cites as genuine, occurs the following passage: "Farewell, all ye virgins; and remember me hereafter, whenever any one of men upon the earth, any hapless stranger, may come hither and inquire of you, 'Who is, in your opinion, the sweetest of the minstrels that dwell here, and with which of them are you most charmed?' Then do you all answer, with the utmost cheerfulness, 'A blind man, and he dwells in rocky Chios.'"

By the way, dear reader, when you visit Rome, fail not to see the old bust of Homer, a grand, majestic head, the sightless balls at rest, in the fixed calm of resignation to the greatest earthly ills. Forget it not, I pray you. Once seen, it will be remembered ever after.

In this Jewel of the East, named the "Crown of Ionia," beautiful sculptured stones are occasionally wrought into modern houses; fragments of temples and ruined fanes of the Byzantine period, hinting of the lovely dead and gone religion which had its devout worshippers when the deathful sirens sang along these shores. Corners of exquisite marbles are scattered about the hills, piercing the burnt-out soil, and, could we dig, doubtless fluted columns and exquisitely carved capitals would be unearthed, bearing great histories and teaching deep lessons. If you have a taste for research and love to copy inscriptions, you find something to repay a weary and dangerous tramp over the volcanic hills. There is much unexplored territory and unnamed "diggings," that would well reward the miner who might be privileged to set up his claim and push his work with diligence and intelligence.

Stately and solemn cypresses mark the Turkish burial-place on Mount Pagus, and here ruins trace the outlines of fortified cities, populous and strong, which have perished from the face of earth and the memories of men.

I will not weary my beloved by telling the many vicissitudes through which the Queen of the Levant has passed, -- how the Ephesian and Æolian Greeks battled for it; how it was attacked by Gyges, the king with the ring (which story with difficulty I suppress); how she has suffered by fire, earthquake, pestilence, by siege, famine, flood, and plague. It was the "pearl of Asia," and passed from hand to hand, the spoil of many victors, long before Columbus sailed over the ocean blue. In the Greek period it was called the "Forest of Philosophers," the "Museum of Ionia," the "Asylum of the Muses and Graces." The battles and sieges of Saracens, Crusaders, Genoese, Turks, battered the old walled city; and phantom images of vast power may easily be invoked by the imaginative traveller.

The dead of many centuries rise and walk abroad at his bidding, sunken ships sail up again, and spectral armies land on the sunny shore. Phoenician adventurers fought here, and many heroes passed this way when the Pillars of Hercules bounded the known world. They bore swords that flashed like Excalibur, and suffocated under chain mail and cloth of gold, -- conquerors bound for the Holy Sepulchre, like Macbeth, bloody, bold, and resolute, ready to do or die for the Cross. Among them were princes of high courage and undying devotion to the Crusades; chivalrous and haughty nobles, whose defiant boast was that, if the sky were to fall, they would uphold it on the points of their lances. Minstrels and troubadours hymned the praises of leaders whose word was victory, whose eye was the bright star of battle and conquest; and wherever harp was heard and sword worn, the fame of the princes was chanted, with vows to plant the banner of the Christian on the walls of Zion. She who wound garlands for helmets worn in such cause was blessed among women; and at home, in her bower, little could the high-born maiden understand how the iron host, with spears glancing, plumes dancing, standards waving in the pride of unconquered intolerance, might fail to make a speedy conquest of Palestine.

The high courage of steel-clothed nobles, riding the heavy steeds of the West, sunk under burning sun and sand against the wiry Asiatic horsemen, all brawn and muscle, mounted on horses called the winged, which every true believer knows were a gift of the Prophet himself to the blessed Ali, his kinsman and lieutenant, well called the Lion of God.

Turn to the historians for records of all the changes which have befallen the finest city of the East after Constantinople. For half a century it was held by the Christian Knights of St. John, of Jerusalem, and in that time twice besieged by Sultans Amurath I. and Bayazeed I., they leading their armies in person. It held out, this glittering prize, against the Ottoman Empire till Timour came, in 1402. He besieged the city, then handsome, regular, and well built, in fifteen days had a mole thrown across the harbor, which cut off supplies and brought the Mongol troops close to the seaward parts of the place. The land walls were undermined, stupendous works constructed, from which the besiegers mounted the battlements, and Smyrna was carried by storm, despite the heroic defence of Christian knights and citizens of Ephesus, who took to their galleys. This scourge of the earth, who shed more blood and caused more misery than any other human being that was ever born upon it, then ordered a general massacre of the inhabitants of the devoted city, and they were slaughtered, without mercy to age or sex. The Tartar hordes from the siege of Sivas (where the conquered Christians had been buried alive, their heads tied down by cords lashed tightly round the neck and under the thighs so as to bring the face between the legs) were ready for more blood. Their insatiate thirst was yet unslaked, and they were let loose on Giaour Smyrna. The records of that butchery are like the frightful remembrance of some ghastly dream. Yet he was only following his customary habit. Timour would slay every male of a tribe, and send its women into such distant captivity that its name would never be heard again by the ears of men. To burn, to overpower, to strike to the dust, sow with salt, annihilate, was the aim of Timour, whose name, meaning "iron," represented in the minds of Orientals the resistless force with which he subdued all things. The pompous titles -- Great Wolf, Lord of the Age, Conqueror of the World -- were no empty vaunt appropriated by the man who, in the thirty-six years of his reign, united in one barbaric despotism the sovereignties of twenty-seven countries, and who ruled in the place of nine several dynasties of kings. He countermanded no order once issued, and it was his maxim never to repent and never to regret. He declared that, as there is but one God in heaven, so there ought to be but one lord on earth, and that all the kingdoms of the universe were too small for the ambition of one great emperor. His sword is still shown in the Imperial Treasury at Stamboul.

Let me enrich my page with a few sentences from Creasy's "History of the Ottoman Turks:" "The career of Timour as a conqueror is unparalleled in history, for neither Cyrus, nor Alexander, nor Caesar, nor Attila, nor Jengis Khan, nor Charlemagne, nor Napoleon ever won by the sword so large a portion of the globe, or ruled over so many myriads of his subjugated fellow-creatures. His triumphs were owing not only to personal valor and to high military genius, but to his eminent skill as a politician and ruler. He had such an ascendency over his soldiers that they not only underwent the severest privations and lavished their lives at his bidding, but would, if Timour ordered, abstain from plunder in the hour of victory, and give up the spoils of war without a murmur. He was a generous master; but his cruelty to those who ventured to resist him surpasses all the similar horrors with which military history is so rife. Timour evidently employed terror as one of his principal instruments of conquest, and the punishments which he inflicted on whole populations often show the cold, calculating subtilty of a practised tormentor, rather than the mere savage ferocity of an irritated despot."

It was the custom of this Tartar chief to build a vast pyramid of human heads when his army revelled after any famous victory and capture. The prisoners slain at Smyrna were not in sufficient numbers to furnish material for such a memorial tower on his usual scale of hideous grandeur. But he would not leave the beautiful bay without the usual fearful monument, and he ordered the heads to be placed between alternate layers of mud plaster, thus to swell the height. Says a quaint old historian: "The tower was made after a new order of architecture, composed in part of stone and in part of dead men's skulls, ranged in order like inlaid work, sometimes full face and sometimes sideways."

XVII. ABOUT SMYRNA – PART II

IN the old days, when Smyrna belonged to the Kingdom of the Beautiful Myths, her women were bewitching with graces of person and wily arts inherited from the gods. The modern Smyrniote has a peculiar witchery of her own, which beams from the languid dark eyes, and, in a soft repose of manner, she passes the daughters of men with her fascinations. How idle these women look, sitting in the doors, gazing at the passers-by, with eyes like haunted chambers, unsearchable as midnight, glittering as the edge of the sword of the Prophet! The descriptions made of them years ago answer as well for to-day: leaning out of the lattices, thinking upon nothing, idle as painted pictures, which, indeed, some of them are. Unchangeable except in costumes, they have abandoned the flowing draperies and veiling scarfs of the Orient for the modern French dress; except, here and there, one may see in the rich braids of jet black hair a long stiletto hair-pin of ancient work, or on the low smooth forehead a fringe of pendant coins, reminder of Egypt. There is a strong dash of Jewish blood, showing mainly in the high nose; and the Greek blood, though thinned by an alien strain, beats warm in the people of Asia Minor. Nor have they forgotten the names of the dead classic times. Aspasia and Sappho make a pretence of embroidery, as they look up and down the street from the projecting balcony. Aglaia and Proserpine yet gather flowers in the beautiful, close-walled gardens.

There is a fountain of pure, sparkling water in the centre of the city, and of this there is an ancient saying: "Drink once of this water, and, though you fly to the ends of the earth, you are sure to drink again." It is not in the fountain alone, grateful and refreshing as it is, that the charm of Smyrna lies. There is wonderful fascination in the variety of color, costume, nationality, which captivates the travellers from the West. Along the broad, well-built quay which extends almost across the entire length of the city, you catch your first glimpse of a caravan of camels, -- a long train, each sixth one led by a donkey. Naturally, the Bible days come into mind. Thus came the Queen of Sheba to Solomon, with a very great train, -- with camels that bore spices and very much gold and precious stones. Into this finest port and richest city of the Levant pour treasures from the four quarters of the globe; but our interest is not in the stuffs of France and Germany, it lies in the bales from Persia. An old chronicler of the past century says: "From Persia came two thousand bales of silk a year; medicines, gums, balsams; all sweet spices, furs, and every sort of carpet; the jewels that sparkle on the brow of beauty; the wealth of Ormuz and of Ind; pearls from warm and distant seas;" and a vague, indefinite idea of all things rich and rare is hidden in the brown bales on the back of the unwieldy, slow-moving beasts. They come from the trackless desert, from Bagdad and Balsora, and an Arab directs their march; he is a true believer, and thinks the sword of the Prophet is the key both of heaven and hell; he prays five times a day, and knows an houri in Paradise is waiting to give him the diamond cup of immortality. When he unloads at the bazaars, you may see carpets of iridescent dyes, soft as finest plush, cloth of gold and silver, scarfs of Mecca (the Holy City of the Prophet), the matchless embroidery Arabesque, shawls of Cashmere and India, and muslins like woven wind; but the trickeries and imitations of the European are ruining the genuine merchandise of the Orient. Base imitation coin is sent to this market from England; and little brass Egyptian images are cast in foreign moulds many a hundred miles from the land of the Pharaohs, and offered as *antica*. German mixtures are taking the place of the rose oil of Damascus, the scent of Paradise, and cheap drugs are offered as balm of Gilead and Sharon. The velvety mohair fabrics are numbered among the lost arts. Beware of the imitations, and hearken not to the voice of the charmer, charming never so wisely, in the bazaars of Smyrna.

The genuine relics of this city, six times totally destroyed, are the citadel on Mount Pagus, an Acropolis built by Byzantine emperors on the supposed site of a great Cyclopean city, a Genoese Tower, and remains of a stronghold which, antiquarians believe, was founded by Alexander. To the Christian (and everything here that is not Mohammedan and Jew is called Christian) Smyrna is most interesting as one of the Seven Churches referred to by St. John in his vision on the lonely Isle of Patmos. It is the only one praised except the Church of Philadelphia. Turn to the second chapter of Revelation, and read what the Beloved Disciple wrote to the First Church of Smyrna. The view from the heights back of the city is very beautiful, and the railway to Ephesus reminds us how the West is encroaching on the dead stillness of the East. Near the summit of Mount Pagus is the site of the ancient Stadium, -- a large amphitheatre, like the one in which Paul fought the beasts at Ephesus. It was in this spot that Polycarp died for the faith, in the year of our Lord 166.

The day we landed in Smyrna was St. Polycarp's day, and the *Bulletin de Smyrne*, a newspaper about a foot square, contained the following announcement: --

"Vendredi prochain, 29 juillet, étant le premier anniversaire du tremblement de terre dont la ville de Smyrne a gardé un si effroyable souvenir, plusieurs Smyrniotes ont prié les RR. PP. Capucins de vouloir bien organiser une messe d'actions de grâces, en l'honneur du patron de notre ville, St-Polycarpe, dont la puissante protection nous a préservés du terrible fléau qui a éprouvé si cruellement plus tard la ville et les campagnes de Cliio.

"Les PP. Capucins heureux de pouvoir montrer leur empressement en tout ce qui est de l'avantage spirituel des catholiques de la ville de Smyrne, font savoir que la dite Messe sera célébrée solennellement à 8½, et sera terminée par le chant de l'Hymne de St-Polycarpe et la bénédiction du Très S. Sacrement.

"Veuille le bon Dieu exaucer les prières des Smyrniotes et les nôtres, et étendre toujours sa protection sur notre ville, par l'intercession de notre puissant Patron St- Polycarpe.

"Le Supérieur des Capucins."

Naturally our thoughts turned to the old story, made familiar in childhood by Fox's "Book of Martyrs" and with deep interest we traced the shape of the ancient theatre where he suffered martyrdom. It is the fashion to sneer at these records and laugh at the noble spirit which taught us how to die grandly, to treat the whole story as a myth or a superstition. It is as well substantiated as that Caesar was assassinated, and to deny it is only to betray ignorance and incredulity.

In the time of the Emperor Marcus Aurelius, when Rome was mistress of the world, Christians were cast to the wild beasts of the arena for the amusement of the populace. Roman literature contains no tragedies, because the ferocious slaughter in public places was bloodier than any imagined possibility in written tragedy. It was no entertainment to read of groans and tortures, when they could be seen and heard throughout the Eastern world wherever there was a faction to gain or a province to be conciliated. Polycarp was the first Bishop of Smyrna. His Life, by Eusebius, is the pathetic tale of a gentle, devout teacher, a fellow disciple of the beloved one who leaned on the Master's breast at the Supper.

Warned by those who endured persecution, at the entreaty of his flock he was persuaded to retire to a place of safety, and not needlessly expose himself to danger. Search was made for him, and his hiding-place was betrayed by a child, who was tortured till the innocent little fellow told the secret. Polycarp still had time to escape; but the single-hearted man remained, saying, "The will of God be done." While he was being led out from the cave, he melted, for a moment, the hearts of his captors by his prayers for them. They did not hesitate long, and he was dragged to the crowded amphitheatre, when the games were almost ended. On his entry, a loud voice, which the old man accepted as a voice from Heaven, shouted in cheering tone, "Be strong, O Polycarp, and quit you like a man!"

The haughty proconsul was moved by the august presence and venerable appearance of the prisoner, and the appeal of a wrinkled, time-worn face, shaded by the shadow of death. It may be he was stirred to admiration by the bold, unquenchable spirit, and he urged him, again and again, to recant, obey the imperial edict, and swear by the fortunes of Caesar. The aged saint looked up to heaven, and said, "Away with the godless." Once more the proconsul urged: "Swear by Caesar, and I will release thee. Revile Christ." Calmly the captive replied: "Eighty and six years have I served him, and he never did me a wrong. How, then, can I revile my King and my Saviour?"

Vainly was he threatened with being thrown to the lions or being burnt to death. To every threat, in defiance of every menace, he quietly answered, "I am a Christian."

The old chronicler says that they who looked steadfastly on him saw his face as it had been the face of an angel. A strange light glowed in it, and his body was like that of the Shining Ones, as he stood friendless, in lonely majesty, in the arena. No soft, fair hand in the balcony to fling a rose at his feet, as love's last token; not one of his faithful followers to stand by him. The sustaining Presence was unseen, and it could not fail, like the help of man. That serene, unfaltering courage was from the heaven toward which he lifted his eager and straining gaze. Eyes dimmed with years could yet see in prophetic vision the heavens opened, and the saints, in bright array, waiting with the crown and the palm for those who come up out of great tribulation.

On the glittering page of Gibbon the reader may find descriptions of the Stadium, and the strifes of the parties, the betting, the breathless interest, beyond the mere passing show exhibited to the spectators. What the spectacle was in Rome it was in less splendor wherever her standards flaunted their purple and gold, and the gilded globes blazed in the sunlight. The shape of the amphitheatre of Asia Minor was a horseshoe, the stone benches rising in tiers, like ours in the opera house. It was open to the sun, which here shines with marvellous strength and splendor, except where a vast awning, striped in bars of crimson and white, shaded the seats of the privileged class. The exhibition was free to all, and the student of history knows what a power it was in the empire to secure popularity. The choicest of the gladiators never left the Imperial City; but in such a place as Smyrna there were always combatants of high prowess and world-wide renown.

The stone benches were solid masonry, as though made by the old Cyclopean giants, who used to haunt this spot. Capable of seating many thousands, now all torn away and used for modern buildings, except the *vomitoria*, where wild beasts were kept for the games.

On the day whereof I write, a mighty and pitiless multitude was gathered. The seats apportioned to the vulgar were crowded early; on the reserved seats nearest the oval arena sat the titled and high-born visitors; on the upper tier were the women, jewelled and radiant in costly raiment, and the rich, bright color which belongs to the Orient. Luxurious cushions relieved the long-sitting, and refreshing drinks and perfumes gratified the beauties, who idly fanned and chatted, and debated the relative merits of rival gladiators. There was music, too, the rousing appeal of trumpets, as the combatants swept slowly round the vast level space, in order to allow every eye to scan their brawny limbs and mark their steady nerve. And the interest of the bloody drama was to rise, as the games went on, till the last act and scene were the crowning, exultant life or the mangled death of those who entered the lists. It was an awful and imposing struggle of men, evenly matched, clad in complete steel and bearing ponderous bucklers and pointed swords.

From the records, it appears that this day, the 28th of July, 166, there had been some sort of failure in the day's sport, and the time was spent without the ghastly complement of the number usually slain. The day was declining. The populace was unwearied; roused by the brutish sports, but not sated, though the sand of the arena was spotted with crimson, the life-blood of professional gladiators or it may be of hapless prisoners. Over the merciless crowd was heard a clamor, a roar like the rushing of many waters, the wild outcry for the life of one helpless old man, to finish the day's enjoyment. "Away with him, the father of the Christians, the subverter of our gods, who teaches many not to worship nor adore them!" They shouted for a lion to be let loose against Polycarp. Philip of Tralles, the presiding asiarch, refused to do this, on the ground that the entertainment was ended. Stern officer as he was, he was touched by the exalted heroism of the passive prisoner. In the moment of deathlike silence which brooded over the Stadium, there was not a hand, not even a mother's hand, held out for the signal of mercy and life. Probably there were those present who had heard the fathers tell of the wondrous Man of Nazareth, who taught in anguish and in glory that his kingdom was not of this world, and who was crucified on Calvary. They knew, to advocate the cause was merely to take place by the side of Polycarp, so they held their peace. The people were warmed into blood, and nothing but the death agony could satisfy their lust.

Around the horseshoe curve, swarming with human heads, echoed the cry: "Let him be burnt alive." While the object of this concentred hate stood, Christ-like, calmly praying, they rapidly gathered fuel from the baths and workshops near, the Jews being most active in the work. It was a sublime tragedy. A majestic peace was in the martyr's mien, and it was plain he held all about him cheap as the dust upon his sandals. Possibly he thought some special miracle would interpose, as did the thirty thousand Christians who once fled to St. Sophia and waited by the altar; but I do not believe it. Silently he ungirded himself, and took his appointed place among the fagots. When they were about to nail him to the stake, he said, with the pathos of one resigned to death, "Let me remain as I am; for He who giveth me strength to sustain the fire will enable me also, without your fastening me with nails, to endure its fierceness." Putting his hands behind him, he suffered himself to be bound, and uttered a touching prayer, thanking God, who had counted him worthy the honor of martyrdom for the resurrection of eternal life of soul and body in Christ, and ascribing glory to the blessed Trinity. The fire was kindled; but a strong wind blew the flames to one side, so he was roasted, rather than burned. Upon which the executioner was ordered to despatch him with his sword. When it was plunged into the poor, tortured body, the blood flowed so fast as to quench the flames, which were rekindled; for the Jews were anxious to have it consumed, "lest," said they, "these people should leave the worship of the Crucified One for this man Polycarp." So into the immortal rest he entered. The play was played out. In the ferocious assembly, a mixed multitude, there was a monstrous sense of satisfaction. The desire of sacrifice was satiated, the thirst for slaughter was slaked. The soft Asian twilight shone on a little heap of ashes, holy dust, that was gathered up by a sorrowing band of his faithful followers, and buried in a spot of which the tradition has been kept unbroken from that day. We know we are on the place of the martyrdom, and close to his tomb, which is almost at the entrance of the Stadium. It is still visited with devotion by Greeks of Smyrna. The hillside where that precious dust was laid rises to the southeast of the city, and a sentinel cypress-tree, straight, tall, and unbending, guards the sacred shrine. So let it rest till the angels of the Resurrection shall gather from the four winds of heaven the holy dead who have died for the Lord.

That life did not pass like the shadow of a cloud, the dream of a sleeper. The light kindled in the arena has never been extinguished in Giaour Smyrna, and it never can be, for the Truth itself has said, "Heaven and earth shall pass away, but my word shall never pass."

We are nearing the great city of the Crescent and the Star. The reader who has so kindly journeyed with me thus far will admit I have refrained from the cheap pedantry of guide-book wisdom, and from loading down with useful information, -- temptations which easily beset the traveller. Gracious presences have hovered about me on the way, as in the grand pictures cherubs circle the Madonnas with wings invisible.

I have tried to be agreeable; only this. If a dark day has been brightened, a dull hour cheered, a tired mother beguiled of her cares in homes my feet may never enter, tell me, O beloved, for 'tis to you I have written these messages. Good-night.

XVIII. POSTSCRIPT

WHEN we had been about six months in Constantinople, one day we four were straying through St. Sophia's. It has not the charm of St. Peter's or of Westminster Abbey, but there is a ponderous weight of history on the gloomy old mosque, enough to make it a favorite haunt for Antiquary, and after a few hours of sight-seeing we usually drop in there an hour or so. The small boy who picks out bits of stone and glass from mosaics on the walls had met us and made us his own, and we carried handfuls of souvenirs for far-off friends to hang with other endearing young charms on slight chains.

Said Antiquary, didactically, as we paused under one of the great cherubim in the angles of the arcades: "This mighty fabric, so shaken yet so enduring, seems to me the best type of the kingdom of Mohammed. Made of elegant material and of tremendous extent, capable of holding twenty-five thousand persons, the collected robberies and spoils from Troy, monuments from the Greek Isles, from Athens, from the Temple of the Sun at Baalbek, and heathen shrines where 'the gorgeous East with richest hand showers o'er her kings barbaric pearl and gold'-- "

"And what a bother to try and remember which is which!" broke in Thalia.

"To some persons," retorted the historian, with a satiric bow. "I was about to say," he continued stubbornly and oratorically, "with all its strength unsightly without, in its clumsy props against earthquake and time, -- crutches for the decrepitude of age. The interior, of rarest workmanship, in dimness and dirt, a squalid magnificence; the costly marbles of the floor overlaid with filthy matting and carpets. Look at the colossal columns from Heliopolis, out of line, banded with brass and tilting uneasily, suggesting the tottering sick man, tenacious of life, who is not going to die suddenly, as the Russian Emperor once fondly hoped, and so settle the long unsettled Eastern Question. Then this wonderful, this matchless dome," he pursued, warming with his subject, -- "its arch airy, graceful, as the blue arch above it, -- builders say it may fall any moment and crush the faithful at prayer below. Well are they named the faithful, intent on their worship, not noticing us any more than if we were so many ants. And to think this very hour all may go to pieces, like the so-called crumbling Ottoman Empire, which has a powerful adhesive quality of its own, and lasts, though swept by tempests of armies, fenced by sleepless foes without, betrayed by traitors within, -- lasts in spite of empty treasury and bankrupt credit, cheerless, despairing, but not quite exhausted."

"Precisely; and having held together at this pitch through centuries, the tough old concern may hang on many generations to come. They have the same saying of St. Sophia that they had in Rome of the Coliseum, 'While stands the Coliseum'-- you know the rest."

"Yes," answered Thalia, smiling brightly; "it's one of the few pieces of guide-book wisdom I do know. The placid Turk serenely waits for the decree written in the fatal Book of Destiny, and is happy so long as he has a sunbeam to prop his roof. -- But who are these?" she suddenly exclaimed, interrupting herself.

"You have the youngest eyes. Tell us."

Across the immense space, in shadowy perspective, we saw a gentleman and lady walking so very slowly we said at once, "Lovers, whoever they be."

When they reached the dingy corner under the women's gallery, where the six green jasper pillars from the Temple of Diana at Ephesus are pointed out to every tourist, we marked the figure of a little lady who in the obscurity and distance showed hardly the proportions of a child. Suddenly she reached up on tiptoe, and gave her companion a swift light tap on the cheek with her finger tips. The movement said, plainly as whisper in your ear, "My fingers kiss you."

"There is but one girl in the world," said Thalia, "who would dare make such a gay gesture in this sepulchral spot; my mosaics against that Egyptian Scarabaeus you are so proud of, that is Regina Atwood and the twenty-fourth Senior. As I live," she continued, in delight flushing rosy red, "there's Uncle again, tagging along with hat glued to his head as usual, and carrying the same ridiculous handbag."

"You notice he follows a good way off, so as not to be *de trop*, the third person not wanted. I always told you Uncle had fine instincts."

"How glad I am to see her again, and to know she is really married!"

"How you do jump at conclusions, my Thalia!"

"And how I do hit them!" she ran on positively. "Look there! now the careful Uncle is wrapping the striped scarf round her throat, as well he may in this damp cavernous hole, knotting it in a big lump at the back of her neck, just like a man. Now she pulls it round under her chin. I can't see her dimples, but I know they are chasing each other over the sweet child's face as she laughs at his awkwardness. That change in her face always reminded me of a flower bursting into bloom. Bless her heart!"

"Amen," said we, fervently.

Thalia waved her handkerchief in high excitement, to the horror of the guard who gravely watches the strangers; but she could not make them see, they were too absorbed, and came forward at a lover's pace, with eyes for each other only.

It was indeed our steamer friend, leaning on the arm of a young man with fresh, eager, handsome face upturned to the ceiling. Through the mystical changing lights of St. Sophia, she looked evanescent and ideal, as though one of the pictured angels, hidden under the whitewash of Mohammed the Conqueror, had floated down to rest her folded wings awhile.

It *was* the twenty-fourth Senior, and they were married. The Paradise of Love about them, radiant with the bloom and glow of youth, the beautiful pair shone in that dreary waste fit representatives of the bright New World which is Hope's own.

About Susan E. Wallace

The daughter of a prosperous Hoosier businessman, Susan Arnold Elston dramatically influenced her life by her choice of Lew Wallace as her husband. A woman with a gift for writing, she used her talents as she followed Lew to his different military, political, and diplomatic assignments as they opened new and exciting worlds for Susan. She recorded her impressions of these new experiences in letters and essays that were compiled in book form three times. Her first book published as a result of her essay writings, *The Storied Sea,* details the travel experiences and people she met as she travelled with Lew to his post as Minister to the Ottoman Empire in 1881.

Susan moved through life as a woman of great intellect, as the wife of a famous American, and as a keen observer of human history. With great wit and eloquence, she was Lew's editor, companion, and inspiration. Their love lasted for over fifty years of marriage, and the dedication in Lew Wallace's masterwork, *Ben-Hur,* is a loving tribute to her.

Made in the USA
Monee, IL
14 July 2021